Wild Justice

Wild Justice

Memoir of a Forensic Psychiatrist

WALTER A. BORDEN, M.D.

ISBN: 1530625750
ISBN 13: 9781530625758
Library of Congress Control Number: 2016905082
CreateSpace Independent Publishing Platform
North Charleston, South Carolina

Acknowledgement and Dedication

THIS HAS BEEN a long journey, aided by my colleague and wife, Edene. She keeps me centered. Sons Jonathan, Richard, and Peter grew up listening to some gruesome but interesting, they say, discussions at our supper table. They were patient listeners, who added another dimension to my views. Rick, a lawyer, gave me new insight into Oliver Wendell Holmes, Jr.; Peter told me after listening to my rants at the dinner table, the title should be "Wild Justice;" Jon, a neurosurgeon and true scientist provided encouragement and input. My perspective was enhanced by my brother David, who was a Connecticut Supreme Court Justice.

Revenge is a kind of wild justice,
which the more man's nature runs to, the more ought law to
weed out; for the first wrong, it doth offend the law,
but the revenge of that wrong, putteth the law out of office.
—Francis Bacon

Words are the physicians of a mind diseased.
---Aeschylus

There is a point at which even justice does injury.
—Sophocles

Contents

Introduction

"SENSELESS SHOOTINGS---MOTHER KILLS her baby." The headlines scream. We shudder. Is violence today some mystery shrouded in dark evil? Does it come from "the inner city," drugs, too many guns, broken families, or moral breakdown? Is it a new kind of plague? Will we be infected? Politicians demand solutions, but politics get in the way. They call for punishment as a solution. Can we find a solution to a plague without knowing the cause?

For a long time, I have been asking the question why we humans are so destructive and self-destructive, and in so many ways. It's one reason I became a psychiatrist and then forensic psychiatrist.

There are many academic, intellectualized and speculative theories. But this is an attempt to answer the question by going on a search for myself.

I am a forensic psychiatrist (now retired). Our purpose is to assist our justice system, when called on, to understand an individual's mental state when that is a question in a legal matter. The best-known example involves the question of legal insanity, especially in heinous crimes that grab attention.

Most people think of the field solely in terms of those high-profile crimes, but that is only a part of what we encounter. Forensic psychiatrists work with all manner of issues—from child-custody evaluations, to competency to make a will in geriatric patients, competency to stand trial, to refuse treatment, and consent to treatment to name a few. We do juvenile and adult court evaluations including worker-compensation court. We evaluate disability, emotional damages from assaults, motor-vehicle accidents, industrial accidents, sexual-harassment, and PTSD; in short, any situation in which mental state is an issue in a legal case. We also work in prisons for evaluations and treatment as well as consultations with private and governmental agencies.

I want to say at the outset that I consider the purpose of justice is to help maintain order within the humane values of our democracy.

I am a private practitioner. I am not employed by an institution, and only accept forensic evaluations when referred by an attorney. I do not accept forensic cases directly from private parties., but I have consulted in the form of advice to victims of stalking, recipients of threats, businesses who have been threatened by ex-employees, and various situations that require an opinion about dangerousness. In criminal cases I am usually called for the defense, but on occasion, I have been called for by the prosecution. In civil cases such as workplace questions, I hear equally from complainants as well as defense. In all, I consider myself an advocate for psychiatric issues, irrespective of who refers the case to me. In addition to performing multiple interviews and psychological testing, I review all available records, interview family and relevant witnesses, and furnish a written report to the referring agency. I often testify.

I have consulted for school districts, and towns, city, state, and federal agencies, and businesses including readiness for return to work. As an example of what I do, let me tell you about a certain case. A town social worker complained to me that she could not understand why so many children from her town were referred to Juvenile Court Detention. We reviewed the referral process, discovered the gaps, and discussed ways to rectify the situation relevant to a juvenile population. It was obvious that psychological assessment of the juvenile and the family was necessary. We outlined a triage system for referrals. Our juvenile-review board concept involved a system of triage with representatives from the police, community and professionals. The purpose is to deflect entry into the justice system for those who really need mental-health treatment for themselves and their families.

Teaching is a priority for me--from supervising child psychiatry residents in Juvenile Court, to teaching a course in psychiatry and law at the University of Connecticut School of Law, providing training sessions for state and federal probation departments, and to teaching a seminar for medical students about medical problem solving--how to think like a doctor.

I do have a separate treatment practice but do not provide forensic consultation to treatment patients. That would be wearing two conflicting hats. Being a forensic psychiatrist for a patient under treatment is considered unethical by the American Academy of Psychiatry and the Law. Besides, treatment is difficult enough, and that comes first.

When a subject's mental state has been raised in legal proceedings, the rights to privacy do not apply. This is a different situation than that of treatment, where privacy rights prevail. For this book, however, consideration for the feelings of relevant parties, names have been changed. Where content might suggest identification, or where there are significant gaps in available information, I innovated, filling in those gaps based on my experience— a kind of professional poetical license. In instances where I have not been able to interview the subject, my report constitutes a record review. In any event, information that comes out in court testimony is considered public knowledge and is therefore not subject to Health Insurance Portability and Accountability Act (HIPAA) regulations.

Over the course of almost fifty years of practice I have seen most forms of human violence: serial killers and rapists, mass murder, homicide, suicide, homicide/suicide, suicide by cop, and suicide by state. The list goes on and on but I have to mention: assaulters (emotional as well as physical), variations in domestic violence (again, emotional as well as physical) and child abuse. Emotional abuse presents a problem. It can be masked, varied and difficult to assess, but words can cause more psychological damage than a beating.

One of the most difficult situations to unravel is when an individual is violent, even to homicide, towards someone they love. This occurs in families, between siblings, spouses, and the most puzzling of all, when a mother kills a child she loves. That is the most wrenching of all for me. Those cases haunt me.

Purpose: Life Story Narrative

THIS BOOK STARTED as a critique of current psychiatry and the law with an emphasis on the bias against mentally ill women. I selected psychiatric problems involving pregnancy to highlight the issue. As the book unfolded I realized this problem was not isolated. My purpose grew, involving some fundamental issues in both psychiatry and justice.

In psychiatry, the need for a psychologically sophisticated life story is essential, but has been neglected in recent years because it has a narrative form that does not lend itself to numerical expression, and therefore does not fit neatly into statistically based diagnostic structures. The latter may be meaningful to professionals, but I have found when testifying, narrative is much more effective in communicating an understanding of psychological issues. I believe that a fundamental purpose of our specialty is just that, to communicate an understanding of the workings of the mind.

As I focused on life story I thought it might be helpful to include my life story to show how I came to medicine, psychiatry, forensic psychiatry, and my perspective.

Although the substance of what I have to say may involve complex psychological matters, I hope to reach interested readers by describing the development of mental illness in real life-stories.

Other purposes that unfolded along the way: the price we pay for our passion for vengeance in the form of "eye-for-eye justice," for our closing our eyes and wallets while opening our mouths about the abuse of women and children, for our disdain of reasoned understanding of psychology, devaluing emotional life, and for our stigmatization of the mentally ill.

I work within psychiatry, an insider so to speak, but an outsider of the justice system, an outsider with one foot in each camp. I would like to think I have a unique perspective of the complicated relationship between these two institutions. Both have long histories of struggles to maintain their integrity in the face of strong pulls in passions that arise from our primitive origins. Those passions were, and are, enemies of moral civilization. I hope to shed some light on these issues as well.

I

Cultural Problems

JUSTICE AND PSYCHIATRY are subject to our cultural biases. In order to highlight this problem, I selected cases of postpartum-psychosis or other problems around pregnancy because these illustrate such bias. This is the tip of the iceberg.

The laws covering women and children, from being abused, being the victim of homicide or perpetrator, are a mishmash of jurisdictional differences. Psychiatry is not much better. The emotional problems around pregnancy especially have been neglected, poorly understood, and pushed into psychiatry's back room (Connell 2002).

That pregnancy is a time of emotional vulnerability is only now being recognized. "Postpartum Blues" has been the broad, popular brush to cover a lot of suffering. That term has contributed to the denial of psychological issues in women. Denial there, may be a word masking misogyny. Until recently, postpartum psychosis was not acknowledged officially. Because pregnancy and childbirth can trigger a variety of mental illnesses, psychosis with the killing of a child often gets lost in a miasma of diagnoses in a field that likes to keep the diagnosis simple, put in numerical terms, and a society that likes to handle sticky problems by punishment.

Most peripartum women with related mental illness, even to a psychotic degree, are not violent to others. More often the end result is suicide or attempted suicide. It is extremely difficult to get accurate numbers because most cases of significant mental illness go unreported. And most probably never reach a psychiatrist (D'Orban).

And there are obstacles. Callousness toward the plight of children, the discriminatory attitude toward women, the stigma of mental illness, either/or thinking, and quick-fix expectations get in the way of justice as it should work.

From my experience, justice as it should work is not a simple matter. There is, sometimes, a conflict between the spirit of law and the letter of the law. This can also be stated as moral compared to statute law. They are not always identical or in balance. Cultural bias and political winds can shift the interpretations of statute law. In democratic justice, moral law (natural law) is theoretically respected, but statute law, couched as the "word," and said to be what the framers intended, can be manipulated to support ideological agendas clothed in legal language. What rubs me the wrong way is rejecting the social context in which the law was framed. Social context contains information about the intent of the framers relative to humane values, and rejecting the context means humane values are extraneous to law. One can assume statute law's literal words are a definition of law, but that is not the definition of justice. I do not understand how the literal words can fly under the flag of "originalists," but leave out The Declaration of Independence and Paine's Rights of Man which reflect humanistic values as the basis of our justice. In my experience the prevailing definition of justice is state vengeance.

Alexander Hamilton's aphorism in debate over the writing of the US Constitution sums up what I am trying to say. "In Law as in Religion, the Letter kills, the Spirit makes alive."

But there doesn't have to be conflict. In times when humane reasoning holds sway, moral law and statute law are indistinguishable.

A major obstacle to really appreciating mental illness is public indifference. Do we as a society, from seeing daily mass suffering, suffer ourselves from a cultural posttraumatic stress disorder (PTSD) with emotional blunting? I can't really explain our toleration of cruelty and brutality except that our society is not as advanced as we would like to think.

We in psychiatry have a special problem, and like dominoes this has created a problem for our justice system. Why do courts continue to rely on the DSM (Diagnostic and Statistical Manual) for understanding of psychiatric issues despite the fact that it is not a clinical text, and warns that the Manual was not developed for forensic purposes? The DSM does not consider causative factors, except in physical brain problems such as cerebral-vascular disease, varies in value depending on the section, and seems to be influenced by turf and cultural interests. It was developed initially to create order in the language of psychiatric terminology to aid clinicians, for epidemiology, research, and administrative purposes. For those purposes, it is of value.

The original purpose has somehow been transformed into defining the actual clinical definitions of mental illnesses. But it is not a clinical text in the same light as medical and surgical texts. Even then, medicine and surgery, or any other scientific discipline, do not have a single authoritative source; virtually all of science is a work in progress, and the same is true for psychiatry. And for psychiatric understanding the DSM has conceptual flaws.

As Kendler (2016) points out, "if meeting DSM criteria constitutes a psychiatric disorder, why should we evaluate anything but the DSM criteria? This view is deeply problematic. Psychiatry is the inheritor of the richest tradition of description in all of medicine because the features of the disordered mind/brain system that is the subject of our discipline are so diverse, so innately fascinating, and profound in the degree to which they illuminate the human condition.

Part of the process of good clinical care is to explore the experiences of our patients. This helps us better understand their experiences, and this sense of shared understanding can be directly therapeutic. The descriptive process, while it doesn't lend itself to numerical categories, is the way to describe in understandable terms the complexities of mental illness, and, probably, other complex illnesses of the human body." He goes on to emphasize that the DSM is a diagnostic index that has come to be "reified" as the disorder itself. "This is a conceptual misconception. The DSM list is inadequate and descriptively insufficient to include the range of human experience expressed in depression." I would also add many other mental illnesses.

Kendler implicates the consequence of our misconception, and indicates the repercussions on clinical understanding, teaching, treatment, and research. Students of psychiatry and allied professions are getting the wrong message because of what he calls "reification." "Over the years, the DSM list of symptoms has lost its original intent, that is, has become "sacrosanct—these criteria have become enshrined in our diagnostic algorithms and structured interviews—that they approach the tokens of an orthodox faith."

If you think this is a problem for psychiatry, sit in a courtroom. I cannot count the times I have heard prosecutors say that the DSM is the "Psychiatric Bible." The term "Bible" has an impressive impact on juries. We live in a very complex age where it comes to technology, but where complexities of the human mind succumb to the need for simplicity, either/or thinking, concrete or spiritual explanations. As a society, we suffer from a lack of a basic, common-sense understanding of human nature.

Our culture equates "mental" with some vague form of weakness, with a strong "know nothing," anti-science, anti-intellectual, and anti-psychiatric wave that muddies the waters for understanding, from climate change to the need for mental-health services. The water gets so muddy we can't see those who are drowning, that is until there is blood in the water or bodies in the grave. Actually, this wave has made it difficult for many to acknowledge emotional problems. It does appear that psychiatry has been defensive and bent over backward to appear "scientific" but losing some humanism in the process.

The consequences of shutting eyes and ears can end in tragedy or, at a minimum, a life of quiet suffering. Psychiatry has to stay alert to not being swept along with the various forms of denial that include the political winds that are fanned by cultural and ideological influences.

Looking into ourselves has always been difficult; not into the bright places, they're easy to see, but into the darkness where emotional whirlpools twirl, where black holes can swallow us, where emptiness and despair reign.

It is no mystery—avoidance of pain is natural. Trying to explain the stars is puzzling, but not painful. Numbers can be difficult to understand, but it does not hurt to try. The immune system or the circulation of the blood may be confounding, but it is not painful to study them. But it hurts when we try to understand emotions. It calls up our pain. We throw up walls to ward off our own emotional pain. And that can be complicated. There are so many kinds of emotional pain. Even then we quickly close our eyes and hearts.

And there are so many masks covering emotional agony. Flights into distractions like entertainment, drugs, other addictions, and mysticisms, leave a deep unconscious abscess that may be silent but grows slowly.

Those abscesses can erupt later when an outside circumstance strikes a resonant chord with that buried pain. The consequence may be quiet suffering, one or another mental illness, psychosis, suicide or outward violence, including homicide. But a similar process can occur in groups of people leading to war, revolution, genocide, and/or a variety of holy wars.

2

My Journey

My ATTITUDE TOWARD the law undoubtedly was influenced by my family. I grew up in the midst of lawyers, politicians, judges, and blue collar families. My father was a lawyer and Democratic chairman of the fourth ward in Hartford; later he became state senator.. He was an old time political boss which is also a good way to describe his personality.

He was born in the Ukraine of peasant stock, and described his father as cruelly abusive, brutal, and domineering. My father told us of the beatings he got, and vowed to be a different kind of father. He took pride in never touching us—no shows of affection either. He ran away to New York, worked days and attended law school nights. At the time college was not a requirement. Returning to Hartford and settling in the North End, he welded Italian, Irish, Jew, and Negro into a cohesive elective machine. But the merger produced heat, smoke, and occasional fires. The dinner table was a stage for debates (sometimes more than animated) about politics, legal cases, racial and class conflicts, and two interpretations of law. I think my early religious training as more Roosevelt's Democratic Party than Jewish, although I was bar mitzvah at mother's insistence.

Early on I was struck by the fact that for millennia morality, or moral law, could conflict with statute law often put as the letter of the law. The argument considered moral law a universal, based on natural law, while the letter of the law was man-made, therefore more vulnerable to the vagaries of human nature, and susceptible to manipulation by political, legal, or personal agendas. I heard that through discussions of legal cases and an inside view of practical politics. But conflict is not inevitable, as during times of humane reasoning Justice is a balance of substance and letter. Out of the heat and smoke of those debates, however, I followed my scientific inclinations to the path of natural law. My natural curiosity led to biology and medicine.

Looking back, my attitude towards psychiatry was first influenced by growing up in a multi ethnic and racial community. This was the 1940's on Mansfield Street. Before it was a street, it was a dump. My grandfather(Zadie) used to tell me it was a "bad place" He had fled the Czar's pogroms and knew about bad places.

This was the early 1940's and the Nazi's aura filtered around the globe, but for me anti-Semitism was up close and personal. I had classmates and neighbors who worshipped Mussolini and Hitler. They let me know. Father Coughlin infected the airways and my neighbor's minds. The stench from Europe and the Pacific was sanitized by calls to honor, patriotism, and revenge: "Remember Pearl Harbor." On Mansfield Street, we bought it, took it in. War was the game we played, and the play could be hard-hitting. Violence and vengeance condoned and glorified. Sound familiar? And we wonder why we have such violence in society? Revenge stories are pervasive in our culture, usually by the good guys, but that's also what motivates most homicides.

While our house was on Mansfield Street, I lived outside on the street with my street brothers and sisters (Our parents were oblivious--benign neglect.) We were a mix of Italian, Irish and Jew. Today we would be called a gang. It was a crucial part of our identity then. Mansfield street was our sovereign turf. The different streets were boundaries. To our east was Enfield Street with its older bad guys; to the north was Capen Street the start of the Negro world; the southern boundary was a "no man's land" of junk filled lots; west was Vine Street and Keney Park. Further west seemed foreign.

There were negative and positive aspects to our Mansfield Street gang. On the positive side: from forming sport teams, collecting aluminum for the war effort, to clearing one of the junk filled lots and making a baseball diamond, to building a clubhouse from scrap wood, we took pride in our ingenuity and team-work. Our crowning glory was building a pigeon coop and raising Tipplers, Rollers and Homing pigeons. Taking care of them was a team effort too, and brought out some nurturing instincts.

Our northern boundary was Capen Street, the beginning of the Afro-American (Negro back then) section. There was some mixing on the street., but more in school. For the most part relations were peaceful, but there was underlying mutual prejudice, tension and rivalry.

Our Capen Street counterparts also built a pigeon coop. Now Pigeons are unaware of human race problems and the niceties of boundaries. The two flocks would occasionally mix as they circled high above us, violating border gang rules. Capen Street felt robbed. Mansfield Street felt robbed, A race riot erupted—over pigeons. That resulted in what I later called the Pigeon War. Fortunately, guns were not available then, but rocks were. The police eventually intervened and negotiated a peaceful settlement—a good example of what police involvement in the community can do. We came to respect the police.

Our differences faded as we reacted to those "foreigners" to the west of Keney Park. We were convinced they looked down on us. And we heard about those enemies further away in the boondocks of West Hartford, Avon, and Farmington. They made occasional forays into our turf hurling at us from drive by cars the likes of "Dirty Jew" and "Nigger." The slurs helped glue us together.

There were exceptions to racial divide. A Capen Street classmate, stopped by and we often walked to school together. Another classmate and best athlete and singer in our Vine Street school, Arthur Sutton, taught us Civil War songs, and gave me a start in football as a runner. That was added to my identity, and carried me through elementary school, high-school and into college. I am indebted to Arthur. There was mutual respect.

Later, in Weaver High School, black and white forged strong bonds on athletic teams, while displacing aggression to the playing fields. Now there was a minority mix allied against those WASPS to the west of Prospect Avenue. The aggression was not entirely displaced. I remember a rally before a game against Hall High of West Hartford when uncontrolled fighting erupted, the police were called, and we were referred to Juvenile Court. That was not the only time I was referred there. It's ironic that many years later I would become a psychiatric consultant to that same court.

Negative aspects of gang mentality prevailed on our street. Macho honor was fundamental. Might was right. And, there was a code; if anyone attacked or insulted family, there had to be retaliation, and like with nations the result was vicious cycles with the retaliation usually far in excess of the original insult. Another part of the retaliation code involved a younger brother being picked on. My younger brother was rambunctious, and I often got the call, "take care of David." The price of living up to our code was emotional as well physical bruises. At home I also tried to take care of David by shielding him from the abuse that my sisters and I received.

On the street, I was the youngest and smallest of the gang. There was a pecking order—I was bottom rung. There were some bad apples, bad guys who bullied, humiliated, and degraded any one weaker. I got beat up, down, stepped on, literally pissed on, encircled by gang members, held down, helpless and had my pants pulled down. I felt sickened, diminished and violated. Shame closed me in and closed me off from people.

There was an additional problem. The Borden's were the only family with a professional father. Nothing was said directly, and we lived in a three-family house like everyone else, but I sensed that set me apart, and added to my need to prove myself.

I had another problem that set me apart. I couldn't read. I was labeled "retarded" until dyslexia was discovered. It took me many years to free my internal self from that label. School was a dark place for me. Failure haunted me, and turned me away from trying to learn.

For my father, a "retarded" son was unacceptable. Frustrated, he'd shout, "stupid---dope---you'll never amount to anything." His form of showing disapproval was humiliation. My mother was different. She also came from a poor immigrant family, but her father, a cobbler, was a kind man who showed some interest in me. Mom's family was musical. She was a self- taught pianist; her sister Fannie, and Sybil's mother was a sing; a brother was a drummer.

She tried hard to help me, but violin lessons (another brother played his way through medical school with his "fiddle") was more failure. I had absolutely no talent. She got me a dog. I loved Rusty, but then my eldest sister insisted that Rusty go. That was the same year we gave up the violin, and I stayed back in school. "Retarded' was in the air.

I later realized that my father's emotional abuse of my sisters poisoned our relationships. I cringed at witnessing the abuse of my two older sisters. I recall how he cruelly put them down whenever they showed pride in accomplishments. I knew how they felt---his abuse was gender equal. He seemed to react aggressively at other's show of ability—he had to tear them down. My mother was depressed and unable to protect us. She, actually was a highly competent person. Mom organized and ran all his political campaigns---the power behind the throne, as long as she stayed behind. The one person in the family able to be close to me was my older cousin Sybil. She was a life line.

On the street, I had to fight to keep my head up, to survive, to earn respect, my own included. There was an unforeseen benefit. I learned to fight and to run—fast. I watched Willy Pep (ballet in the ring) train in Keney Park, and learned his moves. I became will-o'- the-wisp with a football---and determined. Fear can do that.

I lived a double life. In school I was slow, shy, scared. I felt bad and worthless. Outside in sports I excelled and thrived. My self-esteem grew.

One day a teacher told us our new classmate, Rebecca, had just escaped from Hitler's Europe. Miss Brown said we were to be kind and welcome her. It was her first day with us in the school yard that a problem surfaced. My best friend at the time was, Mike, a Negro. It was recess and we were all milling around, but Rebecca was off by herself. Suddenly, out of the blue, Mike went up to her and yelled, "dirty Jew---". I exploded—not thinking. From deep inside something rose up. I found myself punching—don't know how many times. Saw red blood on brown skin--Mike on the ground. I felt sick to my stomach at the sight. That image still haunts me. It was the end of anyone abusing Rebecca--and a friendship. But it was also the beginning of the realization how an unexpected trigger can set off an explosion when it strikes a sore-spot deep inside. That's what happened to me, but also apparently to

Mike. For Mike, it might have been something about Rebecca's situation, her fear and her setting herself apart that day. For me it was witnessing humiliating emotional abuse from someone that I couldn't believe do that. My guard was down.

Out of that melting pot and pressure cooker I learned empathy, perseverance, a sense of responsibility, a growing sense of my worth, the importance of doing the right thing even at painful cost, and an appreciation of hidden strengths. What I appreciate most professionally and personally is seeing people stick to their values despite pressures to abandoned them, and overcome their difficulties in surprisingly unanticipated ways. It takes time, effort, and being open minded. I also learned to appreciate the help I got from those who saw some value in me.

Mike D'Onofrio, who later became a highly-respected detective in the Hartford PD, taught me how to ride a bike. He called me a "tough little shit." Mary Finn stormed into my life in Junior High. She taught Latin and English. I felt I had no business taking Latin—it scared me—going to be another failure, but Mom and my cousin Sybil pushed. They had visions of me going to college. Dad wanted me to learn a trade.

You could hear Miss Finn marching down the hall, heels clopping on the hardwood floor. She was little, a sprite of a woman, but a huge presence—if character had height, she was Mt. Washington--a spitfire in boots—and a great teacher. Miss Finn made Latin and English interesting. Written language became people, personalities and their stories. Language came alive. With me she was demanding, persistent, insistent that I try. She appeared tough but I sensed kindness at her core. She wouldn't let me fade into the background. I thought she'd have made a great coach.

And then there was Merrill Strong, our gym teacher. That's his real name—couldn't be a better fit. Iron-grey hair parted in the middle, a bulldog of a man, a former city handball champion with iron hands and a steely spirit, he was old school. He was tough and inspiring. He instilled values--discipline, the importance of training, teamwork, and, always take care—strengthen body and mind.

Somehow, he saw something in me. Now basketball was not my game. I was fast on my feet, but had no eye, couldn't shoot. Mr. Strong said I was leadership material—I thought he was making that up. He picked me for the

Jones Junior High basketball team. We won the first City of Hartford Junior High City Championship that year. He had me play what he called "layback guard—play defense, don't go over half court, and don't shoot." I wasn't an important part of the team, but, that Mr. Strong believed in me was better than anything. He helped too.

In high school Melvin Crowell taught English. He picked up where Mary Finn left off, only very different in style. Short, slight, soft-spoken, precise, with a twinkle in his eye, he had a corny sense of humor. A worn tweed jacket was his badge. He looked the wispy college professor he'd been. Mr. Crowell opened me to a new language—metaphor. I missed out on my mother's music genes. But metaphors struck a resonant chord—or, more accurately, made the chords resonant. Feelings could be connected to words that sang understanding. That was Melvin Crowell and Sybil. She too became an English teacher at Weaver High School.

By my senior year, I was able to write an essay that was picked for consideration at graduation. The title: "Iron Curtains, Mental and Physical."

But there were still those who, for their own reasons, tried to knock me down. My high school guidance counselor was a graduate of Amherst College. He advised me not to apply there. "You will never be admitted. That's not a place for you." In football one of my assignments was to cover punts. When blockers tried to block me out I learned to just run past them. I called it my "keep your eye on the ball and run past the blockers" principle. I applied to Amherst.

The Dean of Admissions at Amherst then was William Wilson. He told me, "Walter, you do not have the grades for admission, but I got reports from a sports writer in Hartford that you have potential. If you do really, really well on the college boards, we'll see." I did really, really well. He took a chance, and gave me a chance.

The future opened for me.

From Hartford's North End to Amherst College. The central organizing principle of the curriculum then was historical perspective. Since every subject had developed over time there were stages of development with each stage dependent on and extending the depth and breadth of the preceding stage.

That made sense to me. Often there were cross-links between subjects at various levels to make mutual influences. Examples include music and math; geometry, art and culture; history, psychology, drama and literature. Evolution included the biological, historical, and social. For me, this was intellectual fertilizer.

Biological evolution can be witnessed in the developing fetus (embryology). If we describe the development from ovum-sperm to infant (and we can), that is a biological history. Embryology, evolution, and history share common principles.

I played football at Amherst for two years, at safety—football's version of "layback guard." Labs got in the way, but John McLaughry, the football coach, was understanding and asked me to coach boxing, fitting it in to my schedule which I did for the next two years—thank you Mansfield Street.

Later while at medical school at NYU–Bellevue, I learned of the importance of having a medical and personal history to understand a patient's medical disease. During my internship and residency, I learned of the need for a clinically sophisticated psychological history as applied to psychiatric problems; one might even call this an "embryological approach." This has been my orientation in psychiatric diagnosis, treatment, and forensic psychiatry.

3

The Bellevue Years

BELLEVUE HOSPITAL WAS founded in 1736 as an alms house, which was another name for poor house (Burrows and Wallace 1998). Initially it housed the destitute, insane, diseased, and other social debris along with a place for criminals. Later, alcoholics and victims of cholera and yellow fever were added. It evolved into a hospital in response to the growing pains of mother New York City. Waves of immigration, epidemics, politics, riots, advances in the understanding of diseases, the Civil War, and the growing awareness of public-health factors contributed to the development of America's oldest public hospital. But the course has not been smooth. Bellevue became the trash heap for New York City, and psychiatry especially was trashed by popular media.

In the early 1900s, Bellevue became the euphemism for degradation and death. It was filled to bursting with the abandoned, abused, alcoholics, the homeless, the insane, the diseased, those approaching death, and the gutter dwellers— "the dregs."

It was founded on the keystone principal of never closing its doors, of accepting all comers without regard to ability to pay, ethnicity, race, social class, or bed availability. From the beginning, this made the hospital the "dumping ground" for all other municipal and medical facilities for their unwanted patients— "the dregs." That Bellevue became a "dumping ground" is noted in Oshinsky's *"Bellevue: Three Centuries of Medicine and Mayhem at America's Most Storied Hospital,* (2016). I can attest to that. As late as 1957 to 1958 while a medical student on the medical and surgical wards, I personally cared for patients recently transferred ("dumped") from uptown hospitals with IVs and/or catheters still in place. They were invariably hopeless cases in the process of dying, statistically embarrassing, among other issues, to the dumping hospitals. Oshinsky's book is an excellent history of the hospital, but also of NYC and the medical, social, and public-health issues involved in the development of health care.

Bellevue was the first to open a women's nursing school, first to have a children's clinic, first center to have pediatric and child psychiatry departments, first to establish a teaching hospital, first to establish a maternity ward, first to develop an ambulance service, and first to establish a connection to a medical school. The office of Medical Examiner had its beginning in Bellevue, and the Howard Rusk Rehabilitation Institute, a pioneer in rehabilitation medicine, was part of the Bellevue complex. The hospital has a prison ward and a city court. The horror stories made into legends by movies give a distorted picture. True, privacy and comfort was sacrificed for good medicine. But Bellevue has been the final safety net for NY's neediest.

Yellow fever and cholera epidemics, typhus, typhoid, impossible overcrowding, and advances in medicine led to a move to a mansion, Belle Vue, in 1852, and then expansion in 1912 in the midst of new waves of immigration. As best as I can gather from its checkered history, this structure became the Bellevue Hospital Center.

I matriculated at the NYU School of Medicine in 1954. The catchment area, the term for the area from which patients are drawn, was Forty-Second Street to Houston Street, river to river, the heart of Manhattan.

What was medical school like there? I was consumed. It was medical boot camp. I learned medicine, the realities of life on the underbelly of NYC, and the overwhelming miseries that plague many people, wrapping them in disease, suffering, and death.

The old lady, as I tend to think of her, has been replaced by an up-to-date structure, and the clinical medical school is now in the modern, sleek NYU

Langone Medical Center Hospital next door, but the umbilical cord remains connected to Bellevue Hospital.

The structural organization of Bellevue was of Civil War vintage. The "wards" were long, open rooms with beds down the sides and another row up the middle. More were added during times when available beds were filled. Movable screens could be wheeled in to accommodate privacy, but took second place to immediacy. A basic principle, bedrock of Bellevue culture was, never turn anyone away. She was a proud, old lady.

Ward A6 chief resident, Tony Morraco, brought our team of four newly minted third-year med students together before we entered the hallowed ground. This was our first clinical rotation. (The second year of med school had ended just three days before). He pointed to a plaque over the entrance, "*Illegitimi non carborundum.*" Tony translated, "Don't let the bastards wear you down." Later we were to learn that the bastards meant disease and death.

Dr. Morraco was short, swaggering, swarthy, round, and with bluish stubble that defied a razor. "This is real—these are real people. Some may call them the dregs of New York but not by me—and not by you. You guys wear shirts and ties. I don't have to tell the women how to dress. And no first names. Every patient is a Mr., Ms., or Mrs. The operative word is respect—for them, not you." Tony was great. This was a wonderful start.

He explained the Bellevue culture. This was a military-style hierarchy. The chief resident of Medicine was the commanding officer, then came the ward resident. Each ward had a professor attending who made teaching rounds where we presented our patients for critique. They were outstanding clinicians and dedicated teachers. But the chief resident and ward residents had full responsibility. This was a public hospital—no private doctors, no private patients. Every patient was a teaching subject. The head nurse of each ward was on the same level as the ward resident. Next came the interns, nurses, student nurses, and nursing assistants. Medical students were at the bottom of the totem pole. We were expected to fill in and do any job. The culture included the attitude—improvise, think out of the box.

Tony gave us a sketch of our official duties. We'd be assigned patients to follow. That meant the patient was "ours," our responsibility. We were to do all lab tests of bodily fluids, urine, blood, and feces as well as doing EKGs, which the interns and residents would read. We'd draw the blood and send it to the hospital lab for blood chemistries. If our patient was sent to another part of the hospital for a consultation or procedure, we were to travel with him/her to ensure safety and appropriate care.

We examined our patients every day and documented the exam in the chart. The exam included repeat physicals, noting changes, careful observation, listening, and noting any changes in symptoms. We had our own night-on-call schedule. We worked with the ward intern during his night duty. Any patient admitted during that time became ours. We covered the ER from the wards. That meant we'd have to drop whatever we were doing on the ward and go to the ER to take care of the patient there. The resident made daily teaching rounds where we presented our patients.

Oh, there was one other duty. Nights on coverage, we had to patrol, as in scrutinize, every visitor, during evening visiting hours—not to be social, but to make sure contraband wasn't being slipped in. Many of our patients were alcoholic and/or drug addicted, besides whatever other medical problem plagued them. Often their visitors tried to supply them with their toxic cocktails. So—police duty.

Dr. Moracco acknowledged that our status and duties might seem unfair, but he said with a smile, that was the price of the privilege to learn medicine at Bellevue—and besides it saved NYC a lot of money.

Initiation

Clarence Tyler became my first patient. Twenty-six years old, he already had end-stage renal disease from chronic pyelonephritis. Twenty-six was just too young to have developed end-stage renal disease. If there were one thing NYU med students knew it was kidney function and disease a la Wilbur Smith, who for the uninitiated, was kidney maven preeminent.

Mr. Tyler was wheeled into A6 on a gurney from the ER with an IV feeding him a "Bellevue cocktail"—dextrose, saline, insulin, and thiamine. The Foley catheter was already in place. Blood chemistries done in the ER spelled trouble—he looked pale, yellowish, puffy face; swollen belly, arms, hands, and ankles; shallow, rapid breathing; unshaven; blank expression but eyes open. He lay motionless, and tried to answer my questions. He whispered, "Tired...later."

The chart said he was from Pennsylvania, but there was no explanation why he was a patient in Bellevue. My intern said he heard our patient's parents were Christian Scientists, but Clarence's older sister had actually been a resident on A6 several years previously; there was some trouble in the family about Clarence getting medical treatment, and this time his sister forced their parents to have him admitted to Bellevue.

Clarence's wife, Louise, told me he had his first kidney infection when he was eight years old, but since his parents were Christian Scientists they opposed anything to do with medicine. Repeated infections went untreated.

Clarence's sister, Joanne, was the black sheep of the family because of her interest in science. When she went so far as to become a doctor, she was "excommunicated" by her parents. She was "the rebel." Clarence was the good boy. He tried to please his parents. Joanne had a running war to get medical treatment for her brother. She lost most battles until now, but now was too late. And Louise was seven months pregnant. My patient's kidneys were failing. With no reserves, Clarence had months to live, at best.

"Treatment" became daily blood draws to monitor kidney function, but not much else. A low-protein diet was started in the hope of reducing a rising blood ammonia level. A downward spiral. Helpless, both of us. Treatment was really palliative care long before that term came into existence. I fed, bathed, and watched over him. We connected. Our hope held on by our fingertips. To myself, I made the goal to keep him alive to see his child born.

I failed.

Mideast tension

One day, yelling and screaming erupted. And it seemed to be a mixture of languages. I recognized one as Yiddish. I saw two patients, emaciated old men with white beards, white sleeping caps, wrapped in sheets like shrouds. They looked so much alike, they could have been brothers. Both were too weak to get out of bed but lay facing each other, screaming. The one on my right was an orthodox rabbi, Maier Saloman. His neighbor was a Moslem imam, Mohamed Abdul. The rabbi had lived through Auschwitz, turned to alcohol, and was now dying of cirrhosis of the liver. The imam also was near death from cirrhosis, cause unknown. Even so, old hatreds gave them the energy for at least one last fight. We had to separate them, and do it with political tact, not showing favoritism by moving one and not the other. We conferenced. Decision made. The rabbi was put in the middle of the left row, and the imam was put in the middle of the right row across the room. It was a two-bed-state solution.

Later, when the dust settled, I asked Maier what the fight was about. He said it was about God. Mohamed had tried to comfort him by telling him their gods had different names but were the same, wanted only good, and there was a higher purpose to man's suffering. This made Maier furious—his god perished in Auschwitz.

You didn't even ask

The chart said thirty years old, but she looked sixty. Sandra McMullen was a heroin addict. She was a skin popper. Arms, hands, and feet were riddled with tracks. I tried to start an IV, but as the needle touched her skin, she went stone stiff, her back arched, and she screamed. All her muscles cramped at once, throwing her head back. She was rigid and unable to breathe. The resident said, "Opisthotonos." She's in tetany. We have to trach her, or she'll die." He nodded to the intern, grabbed a trach tray, took a scalpel, opened her trachea, and inserted a tube.

The ward had too much stimulation. Light, sounds, movement. The slightest touch could trigger her massive muscle reaction. That's the nature of tetany. We put her in a windowless and quiet side room. But she needed constant attention to keep from cramping. She could convulse from the slightest touch, even from the sheets. It would take three to four weeks for the tetanus toxin to dissipate, even with treatment. For that time, Sandra needed our round-the-clock care.

We worked out a rotation schedule. We bathed her, carefully turned her to avoid bedsores, fed her, cleaned her, kept up with input, output, her blood chemistries, and kept that room dark and quiet. This was on top of our regular duties. We were determined to save her life and to defeat death.

And we did. Through tetany, tetanus, and multiple drug withdrawals, Sandra lived. She emerged from that dark and quiet place to the light of day and a new life.

Two months after she was discharged, Sandra's letter arrived. We thought it was going to be thanking us for giving her a second life. But no, she was angry. And she wanted to make sure we knew she was back on heroin. She added a postscript: "Let me die. I have my reasons, and you never even asked." What she meant was, with all our questions about the facts of her addiction, we never asked about her as a person and how she became addicted to heroin, what the drug meant to her.

Death became the enemy

Death became the enemy. Everything had to be tried, no matter what, to keep the patient alive, or so I believed.

Mr. Jones, an eighty-year-old Bowery dweller, was admitted with a massive cerebral hemorrhage. Comatose, dirt-streaked clothes hanging on a skeletal frame, face gray and sunken, emaciated, breaths blowing through dried foam on his lips. I was the first at his bedside. He laid unmoving, unresponsive, eyes open and staring, pupils dilated and fixed. Pulse was barely detectable. Blood pressure was so low I couldn't get a reading. He was in shock.

Had to save him. I started an IV. About to inject epinephrine, I felt a hand grab my arm stopping me. The resident asked me what I was doing. I said he's going to die unless we do something. He looked me in the eye, and shook his head: "No, he's going to die. He's almost there, we cannot save him. You'll only prolong suffering." And then he asked me if I noticed how Mr. Jones was breathing. It was agonal, a sign of crossing into death without return. Message: observe closely and consider consequences before acting.

Another Bowery citizen was admitted. Bone thin, smelling of the gutter, vomit, urine, and whiskey, she was awake, restless, and coughing bloody sputum. Her fingers were cigarette stained except for thickened bluish fingertips (called "clubbing"). Her muddy eyes roamed and then suddenly locked on mine. I could see terror, desperation—and pleading—we both knew. Suddenly she went rigid, and then jerking, she had a seizure. The convulsion stopped, and so did her breathing. I went to give mouth-to-mouth resuscitation. Again, a hand grabbed my arm stopping me. "She probably has tuberculosis—there are limits—don't sacrifice yourself. This one's a lost cause---we need you here."

Many patients admitted to Bellevue had tuberculosis along with whatever else they had. Often alcoholic, liver disease and tuberculosis were incidental findings, and not the main reason for admission. Medical students were not immune. We could be lost, one way or another, to tuberculosis. We heard the average was about one a year, and we were warned about contagion. I knew, know, all of that, but I still see her eyes—a contagion of a different kind, that plants its germ deep in the mind.

Improvise

It wasn't all grim. Many, I'd like to say most, recovered, but sometimes a little ingenuity was required.

Bellevue was ancient. The elevators were rickety and known to drop. The windows rattled. One night the rain came down like machine-gun bullets. A flash of lightning lit up the ward, then came a thunderous roar and the ward went total black. There was this old man suffering from pneumonia with wheezing, coughing, and the bed squeaking from his shaking. He was drenched and bone-rattling freezing. The wind and icy rain washed over him through the broken window over his head. There was only one thing to do. I requisitioned tarpaper and duct tape in the bowels of Bellevue and covered the broken window.

Don't be naïve

We puzzled for days over an eight-year-old girl's fever of unknown origin. We did all kinds of diagnostic tests, but nothing. Then finally we presented the puzzle to the pediatric attending. He asked, "Did you check for gonorrhea?" We were stunned. "She's only eight years old; she can't be sexually active." But gonorrhea it was. Then he told us to contact social service to find out what's going on at home. Sometimes thinking the worst is realistic.

Non- post hoc ergo propter hoc

A young woman was admitted with a classical lobar pneumonia. That was easy. Penicillin is the treatment of choice and invariably the patient would be afebrile in twenty-four hours. She wasn't. We waited another twenty-four hours. Her temperature was still 104. We assumed this was just an atypical case of penicillin-resistant pneumococcus pneumonia. We gave her a broad-spectrum antibiotic and sure enough in twenty-four hours she was afebrile. We chalked it up to that new medication and patted ourselves on the back for using it. We presented the case to our attending guru, Saul Farber. He looked through the chart and pointed out that the order for the broad-spectrum antibiotic had never been picked up, and the patient never received it, but she had continued to receive the penicillin. It just took her longer to respond. He added for our benefit a Latin saying, *Non-post hoc ergo propter hoc*: Not after the fact therefore because of the fact. He wanted us to remember that just because something occurred following something it did not necessarily mean it was because of that something. We also learned the importance of the details in the chart—read carefully and don't assume.

Another Bellevue lesson learned.

Anything goes

From the medical students' view, the chief resident of surgery was commander-in-chief of surgery. He ran the show. Of course, there were professors, but our main contact was with "the chief." He was boss. He decided with his lieutenant residents which patients needed what surgery and when, which resident would do the surgery, what follow-up was needed, and when to discharge. His operating principle was to operate, to move patients in and out, and make room for more surgical cases. The object was to gain experience, to learn by doing.

Our chief of surgery was an ex-fighter pilot, a fly-boy—cowboy who swaggered through the Bellevue corridors in his Texas boots, and whose favorite saying was how an orgasm was like a good sneeze, with the long buildup and then that beautiful release. He'd tease the women students by asking them how their sneezing was coming along.

There came an evening when I was on C6 duty with my classmate, Paula. She was married, had two children, and came to med school a little later than the rest of us. She was a wonderful person. I can still see her beautiful smile, and hear her "Oh Walter" when I'd make a try at a joke. Several years later I learned she died. On this particular evening, we expected an easy time because the ward was full. There was no room for any more admissions, which meant no admission work-ups for us.

Onto C6 strides fly-boy, asks Paula if she's been sneezing, then asks if there are any open beds. He wants to operate the next day, and needs an empty bed to fill from the emergency room where there is a surgical case. We tell him all beds are full. There are no patients ready for discharge.

He frowns, pauses, and then lopes down the row of beds. We watch puzzling as to what he's up to. He stops midway down the dark ward. All patients are sleeping. He crawls under a patient's bed. Paula and I look at each other.

How crazy can he be? Then he begins barking loud, like a dog. After a few minutes, he crawls out and comes back to our station, picks up the phone and calls for a psychiatry consult. When the psychiatry resident arrives, he tells him there is a patient who must be psychotic. He says the patient has been saying he hears a dog barking. The psychiatric resident goes to the patient, talks to him, comes back and transfers the patient of psychiatry. The bed is now empty. Fly-boy can operate in the morning.

Learning more than medicine

1957 was a flu-epidemic year. The emergency room was coming apart at the seams. There were long lines spilling out onto First Avenue. Paula and I were called to the pediatric section of the emergency department to help with the triage. When we got there, we saw a long line of patients with children, and we started to push through to get to the examining station.

Paula stopped, grabbed my arm and pointed. There was a mother with a toddler over her shoulder. There was something about the child that caught our attention. The child was blue, was dead—and the mother apparently did not know.

We approached her; I lifted the child from the mother's shoulder, and Paula explained quietly that we're all going to the exam room—she didn't have to stand in line any longer.

Plan B

During third year, I got a job working in the Bellevue blood bank evenings. Ordinarily there was sufficient stored blood to meet the demands, but times were changing. Surgical techniques were advancing. Cardiac and vascular surgery was creating an increasing demand, and there were times when blood shortages became acute. At these times the blood bank called on the donors with known blood types who were needed in emergencies. We enlisted house staff, residents, interns, nurses, and students. I got to know more house staff by their blood type than by their names. There were times when the call to house staff did not meet an acute need, and we would enlist a local radio station to broadcast the need for blood. That usually brought donors out of the woodwork of New York streets.

But there came times when even radio appeals did not meet the need. I had been imbued with the charge—improvise. Any means to meet an emergency was acceptable. When there was just no more blood available, and patients' lives were at stake, there was a last resort.

I'd call up to Obstetrics, explain the situation, and tell them "time for plan B." Husbands of new mothers about to be discharged had to give blood or mother and baby could not leave the hospital. Considering how busy OB was, that usually sufficed. Improvise!

Prison Ward

Bellevue had a prison ward that functioned as a hospital for the city jails. In my fourth year, I chose to sub intern for vacationing house staff. I was given the privilege of "covering" the prison ward meaning that in addition to my regular ward I also had the prison ward. The shocker came when I learned that the intern on that ward functioned more like a resident. We could always call a real resident if we needed, but no resident made regular rounds unless requested.

A patient-inmate was admitted with two broken legs from jumping out of a second story trying to escape the police. Well, I was setting up an orthopedic bed on the prison ward with pipe extensions to be used for traction. I was in the middle of screwing in pipes when this massive tattoo-covered, bald bull of a man recovering from pneumonia came over to watch. He said, "You know Doc, with all those metal pipes we could really do some damage some evening." Without thinking I said, "You're right. I didn't think of that. I'm appointing you as guardian of the pipes." He paused, and then broke into a big smile. "Don't worry, Doc; I won't let anyone near them." There was no trouble.

I learned a lot—how to talk down violent and/or suicidal prisoners, and to pay attention. A young, non-English speaking man kept pointing at his left ear and shaking his head. I couldn't understand the language he was speaking. It wasn't Spanish. I looked in his ear with my otoscope, and there staring at me was a cockroach. This time I picked up the phone, called ENT for a consult and told them, "Cockroach in ear—please remove."

Suicide attempts were a problem in the prison ward. One patient started at the end of the ward, ran to gain a full head of steam, then crashed headfirst into the opposite wall in an attempt to crush his own skull. We had to tie him down.

Another patient carefully measured the distance from the metal rail at the foot of his bed to the floor, tied a bathrobe belt to one end of the rail and the other end around his neck, then keeping his body stiff fell over breaking his neck, succeeding in killing himself.

Be skeptical

People ask me if I became a psychiatrist because of experience at Bellevue. What immediately comes to mind at that question is a lecture in psychiatry where an attending Bellevue psychiatrist presented a "classic case of paranoia" based on a patient with the "delusion" that his wife was poisoning him with arsenic. A few months later when we were on medicine, guess who was admitted with arsenic poisoning? Another Bellevue lesson: don't trust labels, be skeptical, and, again, don't assume what seems obvious. No, Bellevue did not spark my interest in psychiatry.

4

The Rochester Years

*It is more important to know what sort of person has a disease
than to know what sort of disease a person has.*
—Hippocrates

AFTER BELLEVUE, I interned at Strong Memorial Hospital at the University of Rochester. Strong was unique because it offered a two-year rotating internship—six months on each of the major medical and surgical services—including of all things, psychiatry. My interests, then, were a Bellevue legacy: renal disease and cardiology. I was going into internal medicine. Psychiatry was not on my radar, but I figured it couldn't hurt, and it was mandatory in that internship.

There were ghosts from my Bellevue past. Clarence Tyler, Maier Salomon, and Sandra McMullen haunted me. They first rose from my depths when my medical mind was pried open by a brilliant clinician and master teacher. George Engel was psychoanalyst, internist, and researcher. He was ahead of his time—he coined the phrase biopsychosocial, and his research spanned the complex network of influences that can color a life or grow a disease. He highlighted the psychological underpinnings, but also the consequences of medical problems—cause and/or effect. Psychosomatic, but also somatopsychic. People are complicated. Their diseases are complicated.

Engel spoke of the powerful influence that loss and the vagaries of emotional trauma had on health and disease, pointing out the interactions of mind, body, and social context. He emphasized the latter—the social and psychological context at the start of the first signs can often shed light on important factors, and context may help explain exacerbations and response to treatment. Individual lives were very different. One man's trauma was another man's challenge. He taught by doing. We watched his interviews where he brought out patients' life stories and how their emotional issues wove into their health and disease.

His interviews were a life-story journey, Doctor and patient walking that road together. Dr. Engel showed the way with questions, and his patient-partner, not being alone anymore, was able to give him clues as to what was important. Engel's role was to be sensitive enough and know enough to read the clues. He connected the dots—that's also the doctor's job. The shared life story is a road to healing.

As he asked detailed, probing, but empathic questions, I could see him resonating with the person-patient. He helped bring emotions to the surface—and doctor and patient connected. He emphasized relationships, identifications, losses, patterns of dealing with pain, vulnerabilities, and strengths—the life story to fully understand the person and his or her disease. The guide to understanding is connecting the dots—that's the doctor's job and sharing that is emotional transfusion.

When patients repeatedly relapsed for unknown reasons, they were usually considered to be either noncompliant or suffering from some unknown inherent biological problem. Dr. Engel asked about how they were taking care of themselves and what their feelings were about themselves with their disease. He asked detailed, probing, and empathic questions. Were they afraid of dying? How did they feel about death? Had close family members had the same or similar symptoms? If there were deaths, did they watch the suffering? What was that like? He asked questions with empathy but in a low-key way that communicated objectiveness rather than sympathy.

The wall between person-doctor and person-patient faded, and as it did, so did noncompliance.

He emphasized the importance of getting a patient's life history to fully understand the person and the disease the person carried. I came to think of it as walking with the person-patient through his or her life. The life story often sheds light on dark mysteries of illness. Interest in a person's life story is emotional transfusion, and it cements connection.

George Engel was at bottom, medical humanist. He spoke of the powerful influence of personal loss. He pointed out the complex interactions of mind, body, and psychosocial context. What was going on when the symptoms first started? As examples: a loss, divorce, rejection, failure? And what was the context when illness recurred, became worse, or better? He connected the dots. Life story was central.

History is Prologue

John Romano was chairman of the Strong Memorial Hospital Psychiatry Department. He was an imposing, towering figure, both literally and figuratively. Along with Engel, he made Strong Memorial a major influence in medicine and psychiatry. We met with him weekly, but in addition, he made regular rounds where we had to present cases to him, especially our problem cases. Woe unto any intern or resident who could not provide a full life history of the patient, family, and relevant ancestors, as well as cultural issues. He drilled into us the importance of past records, not only psychiatric records but medical, school, military, arrest, legal, and any public record. Dr. Romano was a historian, scholar, and clinician. He taught us that history was medical and psychiatric prologue.

Clarence's life story surfaced for me with new understanding. He told me how he felt his kidney disease was a sin against his parents. He told me how hard he tried to get rid of that sin. Since treatment was confirmation of his guilt, he had to go along with his parents' wishes to protect his soul by denying treatment.

Sandra also came to life again. She told me she was angry because she wanted to die and we—enveloped in our selfish need to prolong her life—stopped her way of suicide. Heroin was how she choked off her mind, strangling the memory image from when she was eight years old—of her mother hanging and twisting. She had never talked about it with anyone, and it was an abscess eating her inside. She couldn't stand the emptiness, pain, and loneliness any longer. She hungered to rejoin her mother in death. We tried to stop her.

Rabbi Saloman returned and told me of the horror that burned his soul, destroyed his faith, and turned his God into the ashes that rose through the chimneys. The smoke and ashes were stamped behind his eyes as agony. Alcohol promised deliverance.

I became increasingly interested in how psychiatry and medicine were intertwined. George Engel, John Romano, Sandra McMullen, Clarence Tyler, and Maier Saloman pulled me into psychiatry.

After Internship

I couldn't start a residency in psychiatry immediately. I had made a commitment to the United States Public Health Service Heart Disease Program, a legacy of Bellevue. My two years in the Public Health Service in Atlanta, Georgia, became a great clinical experience; it introduced me to public-health issues, community medicine, and the social and cultural connections.

One of my assignments was to set up a statewide stroke-rehabilitation program that emphasized rehabilitation in the home by family. This was a unique concept tailored to the rural poverty-stricken setting that lacked medical facilities. Our team of myself, a senior physical therapist, and supervising public-health nurse traveled throughout the Georgia countryside putting on three-day teaching programs for public-health nurses. We trained them in rehab techniques that they in turn would teach family for taking care of stroke patients in their homes.

This was the early 1960s. My first order of business before being given permission to do the program in any county was to meet with the local medical society and convince them we were not a Yankee plot. And I made sure the public health nurse groups we trained were integrated.

I also worked in the Grady Hospital cardiac clinic and the Emory pediatric heart surgery section. Grady was a lot like Bellevue.

I was fortunate. The head of the Georgia State Heart Disease Program, J. Gordon Barrows, was a gifted physician and administrator. He developed one of the first diet studies of heart disease, enlisting most of the Trappist monasteries in the United States, which are vegetarian, comparing them against an equal number of Benedictine monasteries which have a regular American diet. He enlisted the Catholic Church into allowing comprehensive physical exams, EKGs, blood studies, and autopsies. This project went on for some twenty years.

After my service in the USPHS I returned to Rochester, to Engel and Romano, and honed my skills in the psychiatric residency for the next three years. While I was away in the USPHS, the psychiatry department at Strong developed one of the first liaisons with a court: my introduction to forensic psychiatry

Psychiatry and Law

> *It is a universal conviction of mankind that morality is a higher norm than the positive law. This conviction is so universal that law makers and judges continually appeal to morality—The Natural Law*, Heinrich A. Rommen, Liberty Fund, Indianapolis

Mental illness often slips through our safety nets, and becomes entangled in the justice system. In enlightened circumstances justice askes psychiatry for assistance in order to make intelligent decisions.

Where psychiatry and law interface is where a society's attitude toward mental illness is debated. That attitude is also an index of a society's measure of civilization. We don't get a good grade.

In forensic psychiatry the job is not to answer the question of who did it, but to answer why? Or, when a medical problem is mixed with mind, to do some sorting out. Psychiatry's role in the legal process is to concentrate the focus. It's like a telescopic mirror concentrating not light but information. By reviewing all the information, we seek to make psychological sense of what seems chaotic. The adversarial system with direct and cross examination sharpens the focus on motivation and especially intent. What was in the mind, how did it get there, and how did the mental state affect symptoms or behavior?

In rational times, when the question of mental illness is raised, the justice system can be a very good place to learn about mental disease. The legal process, if it can remain free of stigma, either/or thinking, stereotyping, turf wars, and petty politics (a tall order), can be a window into the mind. In court, a person's whole life story can be laid out. Psychology can come to life. The courtroom can become a place to sort out the wheat from the chaff and concentrate the significant information into an understanding of the mind. The psychosocial issues can be integrated with the biological rather than the either/or, psychological vs. neuroscience.

But even the whiff of mental illness is a barrier. Cultural callousness toward the plight of children, the discriminatory attitude toward women, the stigma of mental illness, either/or thinking, and quick-fix expectations limits the understanding of psychiatric issues.

Why I Care

The people who haunt me in these pages suffered needlessly. If someone in a helping profession had taken careful life histories, gotten to know them as individuals and their unique, emotionally toxic experiences, the psychological evaluator then would have a better understanding of the psychological context, a perspective, and certainly of the vulnerability of developing danger to self and others. Directed treatment would then have been possible. This is analogous to many medical illnesses, which do not arise out of the blue in adult life. The doctor has to go back and get a history, to learn there were predisposing or causative factors that occurred earlier in life related to current compounding factors. This has to be explained in a life story narrative giving a better understanding and opportunity for more effective treatment. Tragedy can be averted.

5

Eve
"Somebody Stole My Baby"

Of all creatures that can feel and think, we women are the
worst treated things alive
—Euripides, Medea

SCRAWNY, SOBBING, SIGHING. Greasy, tangled red hair sat atop a face scrunched with pain. I smelled despair. Tears spilled from red-rimmed eyes down splotched, sunken cheeks. Her dress was dirty, sweat stained, and hanging on slumped shoulders. Her hands were white—knuckled, wringing. Fingernails were stubs. She trembled from head to foot. I took in her fear and desperation, could sense her pulling me in—her neediness—and felt an immediate connection.

I have developed a semistructured interview to help people tell their life story, their personal history. I inquire what brings them to the psychiatric evaluation, carefully observing nonverbal cues that may help in starting the interchange. I ask a lot of questions, concentrating on meaningful relationships. If the patient rambles, appearing to avoid dealing with something pertinent, I bring her back on point. My introductory question is usually about significant people, having them described as a person. But Eve didn't give me a chance to start.

She blurted out, "I love my baby. Moving around inside, she was part of me—me—Eve."

She was seventeen and married to Frank. The tale spilled out. I got out of the way to let it flow. "We came here four months ago. Living with Mom and Ruth—when Rachel was born. She kicked us out." Eve looked down. "Mom said Frank raped Ruth, my sister—yeah, he probably did."

At that point I wanted to focus on what happened to the baby.

"Your baby was stolen?"

Eve sighed. Tears spilled. "I took Frank to the factory around seven thirty. Drove along the river road. Rachel was in the car seat. I was thirsty so I stopped at a store for a Coke. I was only gone minutes—got back in the car, turned to check on Rachel. She was gone." Eve stood, legs trembling. "Sick to my stomach, I drove back to the store, and asked if anyone saw a baby. They said no—drove straight to the police---told them somebody stole my baby.

"They found a baby floating in the river, face down—dead. They were sure it was my Rachel. Handcuffed me—said I needed a lawyer—got me Chris—public defender. Chris sent me here."

Chris was a good guy, always smiling; he seemed meek, not the picture of the battle-scarred, tough lawyer he was under the smiles. He was a longtime public defender from what appeared to be a quiet, rural area but actually the site of some grisly crimes. He represented some of the more bizarre and puzzling cases that came out of the hills. He was a puzzle solver and had asked me to help in the past. We respected each other.

"I thought I'd seen it all." I could tell he wasn't smiling; this must be trouble. He laid out the facts: A young woman, a teen, really, went to the police, obviously upset, claiming her baby was kidnapped. She gave them vague details, the gist of it being that the baby was taken from her car while she was only minutes in a convenience store. She denied knowing more and gave them a step-by-step account of her activity that day. She seemed sincere. When she told them about her husband, they began to suspect him. She described him as ice cold, didn't seem to care about her. He gave them a weird story about Eve, some reference to the Bible, being possessed, and that she must have done something to the child. He seemed eager to implicate her.

Chris said the prosecutor was puzzled too. Both thought either Eve was a closet actress hiding something or the husband was crazy, like a fox. Chris sent me the police reports.

I asked Eve about "possession." She told me she knew what they said about her. They thought the devil spoke through her, but she denied it and thought it was ridiculous. She'd seen people in the church speaking in tongues when they dragged her there. They jumped up and down, shouting gibberish. She didn't believe in any of that "nonsense." They accused her of being evil. They lit candles, burned incense, and said they were trying to coax the evilness out of her. "They must be crazy."

Eve denied any knowledge of Rachel's disappearance. She didn't believe her baby was dead and wanted the police to continue the search. "She's out there somewhere. The dead one must be somebody else's." Eve was adamant. She knew nothing. She sat still, her face a blank; soft spoken, monotone; no feelings escaped. But when I asked about the baby, her face broke like a dam, crying. She said Rachel was wonderful, cranky sometimes but a pleasure. She pleaded, "Love my baby—help me find her." Was this barely educated girl a gifted actress?

My first impression: she wasn't acting. But if she wasn't, what was going on? Better yet, what was happening in her head? To get there, I needed to understand her as a person. I needed to travel with her through her life.

How do I assess a life history? After obtaining identification information, I launch into the family history. This is structured with questions about the immediate family members: names, ages, health, and major problems. Then I look for a description of them as individual persons.

"Mother never thought of her as a person. She was wonderful, a saint, cooked whatever I wanted, did everything for me—us."

"Well, what were her ways of discipline?"

"Oh, she had that leather belt. Beat me till I was raw, but I deserved it."

"Why deserve?"

"Don't know. Must have."

"What else was she like as a person?"

"She just hung around."

"Doing?"

"She drank a lot—that's when she beat me."

"What was she mad about?"

"Don't know. Dad, I guess. They fought real bad. He sent her to the hospital."

"How did you feel, seeing them fight like that?"

"Scared. Thought she would die. Terrified. Wet my pants. Still see it in my mind."

"Do you think it affected your relationship with her?"

"Don't know, but scared I'll lose her. Almost did. Last year she was in the hospital with pneumonia. I couldn't visit—too nervous."

We go through the whole family—friends, teachers, anyone who had a significant relationship. Losses through death, divorce, separation, rejections, and how that made them feel is especially important.

They usually start with a superficial description of a parent in idealized terms. Then I emphasize person and start digging, always referring to feelings and relationships. If I am able to read the person correctly and ask the right questions, there is an opening up, and their insides spill out for both of us to see.

I asked Eve to describe every family member as a person, how each of them related to her and she to them. Then I asked, "How would you describe yourself as a person?"

Eve was stunned at that one. "Me, a person? Dirty, stupid me? Don't know—I'm Eve." Her self-esteem was around her ankles.

"Your mother?"

"She was Mom." No more. She probably got no more from her mother either.

So, I had to get a better picture of Mom. "What was her life like?"

That began Eve's life history.

"Mommy was fifteen—pregnant with me. She wanted to get rid of the thing inside, but Grandma said 'no way.' Daddy said I wasn't his—he was a drunken bum, no good—left us because he couldn't stand me, the baby crying. He had huge, bushy, black hair. Voice like a train. Scared me."

She wasn't sure if he was a dream or real. "A ghost—hooded—no face—over me. Looked up over the hood. There was a sunny circle, a tree in the middle, on the top branch a black crow singing. Made me happy. Called him Sandy. Made fear go away."

So much in a few words: unwanted, rejected, abandoned, cause of abandonment, guilty times ten, terrified, reality too much, chaos, flight into what we call dissociation, a fancy technical term for a mental escape from horror—fantasy that becomes reality. I'd heard that from rape victims and others in the midst of horror, imagining they were someplace else. When that kind of mental escape is called up early in development, it gets imprinted—available for dealing with future horror—and can have other consequences. It really is the mind splitting, becoming an escape but also a vulnerability apt to recur in extreme trauma.

Eve had a clearer memory of her stepfather, Jed. He came on the scene after her sister was born. He'd come into Eve's bed and touched her "privates." But she said she didn't feel scared. "Sandy came to me singing. Jed disappeared. Daddy Jed said he'd beat me and make Mommy beat me too if I told." Her mother kicked him out. "She blamed me."

They moved to Grandma's. Grandpa did the same as Jed. She was afraid to tell, and Sandy protected her.

As for school?

"Don't know. They passed me. No time to make friends. The other girls stayed away. I think I smelled. Grandma made us move when I was thirteen."

She met Frank a couple of years later. "He followed me home from the store. Said he liked the way I walked. He was cool. Good talker, good looking, said I was pretty. My tits looked better than the other girls'; he just wanted to feel them a little bit." Frank told her he liked her. That was all Eve needed. She was in love. A "little bit" became a lot more. He bragged to his friends about her. "He passed me around."

Eve missed her period. There was some question about the father, but her mother said she had to marry Frank. Eve was sick, and her moods jumped around. Some days, she felt she could do anything: "Cleaned the house over and over, even the toilet. Couldn't stop." Other days, she couldn't tear herself out of bed. She was so irritable, she'd jump at the slightest noise. Mom made sure she saw the doctor, took the vitamins, and stopped the drinking that Frank tried to pour into her. She said she liked being pregnant. "Made me feel special." Rachel was four months when Ruth told Mom that Frank had raped her. He admitted it. He said Ruth seduced him, and Eve didn't satisfy him after she got pregnant. Whose baby was it, anyway? "Kicked out—had to go up north to live with Frank's mother."

Eve thought she should be happy, new mother and all, but she wasn't. She felt empty but couldn't eat. She was increasingly irritable and confused. She'd go from "high" and very active to "down," almost paralyzed with fatigue. She couldn't sleep, but when she did, she kept waking up, drenched in sweat and shaking. There was some weird nightmare that she couldn't remember.

Eve sensed her mother-in-law didn't like her; there was just something about the way she looked at her. "Then there was the devil thing." Frank and his mother, Alice, kept telling her the devil was speaking out of her mouth, that during the night, they heard the devil coming out of her. It wasn't her voice—it was a man's deep voice.

She said she didn't believe in the devil. "It was their church, never heard of it. They dragged me there—I saw people waving arms and speaking gibberish." She thought Frank and Alice were trying to drive her mad, saying she spoke in tongues too. They took her to the pastor for an exorcism. He told her she indeed had some evil thing inside her and made her repeat chants with lit candles in her hands. She came away thinking he was crazy too.

Eve insisted she didn't know what happened to Rachel. She repeated it over and over, no matter how I asked. She repeated that she never spoke in tongues. She insisted that Rachel was still alive somewhere. Whoever stole her was keeping her.

I met with her and Frank together. Each stuck to his or her own story. Frank insisted Eve spoke in tongues and that his mother heard her too. They heard her speak in an unnatural man's voice, saying he was the devil, the world was evil, and all would die in flames.

I was at my psychiatric wits' end. No, there was another card to play. I had always been very skeptical about the use of hypnosis in forensic examinations. There was too much possibility for distortion and deception through suggestion. I'd seen too many cases where hypnosis was exploited by one side or the other. I'd come to the conclusion that the only way hypnosis might be credible was if it were video recorded from beginning to end, so it could be seen and heard with all the nuances and emotional coloring directly witnessed. I called an expert in hypnosis, doctor H. I explained the situation, and he agreed hypnosis might help. We would do the interview together; he'd do the hypnosis while I ran the video camera. I then contacted Eve's lawyer, asking him for permission to do a hypnotic interview. He said okay but referred me to Eve. She was somewhat hesitant and fearful, but I explained it was something to help me understand her, nothing more. She agreed.

Eve's Hypnotic Interview

Eve fought the hypnosis at first. She tried but couldn't lower her guard. The video camera wasn't the problem; fear was.

Dr. H. first tried a conventional approach. He had her focus on a swinging key while he droned on about relaxing. He almost put me to sleep, but not Eve.

I shared Eve's complicated history, including her mental-escape ways. Dr. H tried again, this time suggesting she let her mind wander to something pleasant, to picture a scene from the past that brought her comfort. He droned again.

"I see Sandy up there. He's come back." Eve slumped, eyelids drooped. She was under. I asked her to go back to the day Rachel disappeared. Eve said she dropped Frank off at work. She was driving home along the river road. Rachel was in the car seat in the back. Thirsty, Eve stopped at the convenience store, ran in and got a soda, drank it hurriedly, and quickly got back in the car and started driving again.

There was a field on the left and trees on the right along the river. She was feeling good, warm; it was a sunny day, but then it started to get dark. The trees, even the leaves, turned black. She found herself slowing the car. She didn't want to—something seemed to take over; her foot was pressing on the brake on its own, slowing the car to a crawl, stopping it.

She was scared; her mouth was dry, and she was short of breath, quivering. She heard something, vague at first, but then a voice, a man's voice, deep, louder and louder, booming. She was shaking, trembling; she felt sick. The voice stormed her ears, her mind. "There's a fire. The world is burning—you have to save Rachel. Carry her."

Eve obeyed. She found herself walking slowly, with her baby in her arms, through the blackness. The voice was thunderous, commanding. "Drop Rachel in the water." She obeyed.

Then the voice laughed. It laughed and laughed at her. "You stupid, dirty girl."

Back in the car, driving home, she turned to check on Rachel—but she was gone.

As Eve went into the hypnotic trance and told what happened, her blank and emotionless mask dropped. Agony and terror swirled in her eyes. Tears spilled out. Her forehead was furrowed, her mouth wide open, her lips pulled back in a silent scream. Mucus dripped from her nose. She leaned forward, body cringing, hands wringing, legs trembling. She was back in the nightmare—and it was real. We were transfixed. She'd brought us with her. Dr. H came to first. He ended the session. Eve awoke with a pounding headache—and absolutely no memory of what she had told us.

I sent a copy of the videotaped interview and my report of Eve's mental condition to Chris. He met at the state's attorney's office with a steely, case-hardened group of prosecutors, investigators, and state police. These were tough guys who didn't trust psychiatry. Chris played the video. There was a long silence filled with unfathomable tension. Chris couldn't tell what they were feeling. They asked him to step out and wait. Minutes later, he was told a plea of not guilty by reason of insanity was accepted. Eve was going to a hospital for the criminally insane rather than to prison.

Eve

Eve's life history highlights several disturbing problems in psychiatry, medicine, the law, and our culture.

I constantly read in the papers and see on TV the question: why? Why did they do such horrible things? This seemingly never-ending question is never followed by suggestions as to how that question is explored. If we look at the usual exploration attempts, we find journalists, but they are usually not trained in criminal psychology. Then there are state investigators, also not especially trained to look under mental rocks. Even forensic psychiatrists can be hamstrung by a narrow focus determined by several factors, including psychiatry's overdependence on the various versions of the Diagnostic and Statistical Manual of Mental Disorders. This is despite the fact that this is not really an authoritative text, although the courts seem to think it is. The DSM does not consider causation, is produced by a committee, has been swayed by popular cultural currents, and is particularly weak in areas relevant to women.

Eve did one of those horrible things that always prompts the question why? She killed the baby she loved.

In this case, the legal process enabled an answer. The examining psychiatrist was allowed to bring a video camera into the prison to tape a hypnotic interview of Eve. More accurately, the legal process enabled the collecting of crucial psychiatric information. The findings were clear, graphic, and obtained in a way that made them unquestionable. She was psychotic, delusional, and responding to command hallucinations. The commanding auditory hallucination made her drop her baby in the river in order to save the child from the delusion of the imminent fiery destruction of the world.

Because the forensic exam was allowed to video record a hypnotic interview, her psychotic state of mind at the time of the infanticide was revealed in such vivid form that it was clear she was responding to command hallucinations and was not malingering. She neither knew it was wrong nor could exert rational control. Lack of understanding and ability to control means she was legally insane and therefore not guilty.

Her psychosis was complicated and did not fit into the usual, diagnostic categories of psychiatry. Postpartum psychosis is not even in the DSM in a clear form. There is an interesting parallel in the very recent findings that the stressor—that is, the trigger—of a PTSD mental illness can also be dissociated and therefore hidden in amnesia.

But for the video recording of the hypnotic interview, Eve would have been convicted of murder. That she was hallucinating and delusional would not have been known, because she had amnesia for the period of active psychosis. Technically, this was a dissociated psychosis occurring in the context of a postpartum mental illness expressed by "possession," as described by her husband. This can be thought of as a cultural coloring to her postpartum mental-illness symptoms. This is a very complicated mental illness and would be extremely difficult to describe in words to a jury.

One picture is better than a thousand words. In this case, ten thousand plus. Aside from the causative factors and the diagnostic labeling, the video of the active psychosis was very graphic, very convincing, even to a highly skeptical audience. It amounts to objective evidence. It also raises the issues of the value of video-recording interviews and the use of hypnosis in forensic situations. Police interrogations as well as forensic evaluations would benefit.

From a practical perspective based on my testifying in many cases where mental illness plays a role, everyone today wants a simple and especially a physical explanation of mental illness. There has to be blood on the floor, a brain tumor, or indications of some genetic disorder, even though the latter still lacks objective evidence as the cause of most mental illnesses. It seems that a family history of some mental illness is automatically accepted as a genetic cause, whereas child abuse from disturbed or malicious parents is ignored. The psychological impact of child abuse is an extremely important issue in understanding mental illness but remains a huge cultural blind spot.

When a woman kills her child in the setting of marital discord, the prosecution automatically considers her to be a malicious Medea, motivated by animosity toward her husband. The irony of that has been lost. To Euripides, the author of Medea, the play was an example of what oppression and brutality to women could do.

This situation is compounded in a postpartum psychosis because in the area of mental disturbances associated with pregnancy and childbirth, psychiatry is a work in progress and is not authoritative. (Friedman, Resnick et al, online Journal of American Psychiatric Association, Child Murder 2005)

Eve's childhood was an emotional war zone. She was unwanted before she was born and referred to as a "thing." I would add that she was treated as a thing for the rest of her life. Her biological father was a mystery recalled in a nightmare that was mixed with reality. Nightmare becoming reality was a theme of her life. In any event, Eve was blamed for his abandonment of the family.

Her mother was also a shadowy but icy figure whose protection of Eve was left to the wolves. Eve was sexually exploited by her stepfather and then by her grandfather.

Exploitation by men became her natural state. On the surface, nothing seemed to show. She was a passive vessel men could use for waste.

But what happens under the surface? Anything? The destruction of her self-esteem is much like being burned alive, leaving smoldering ash that never quite goes out. Something can fuel the smolder to ignite, even explode. For Eve, becoming a mother was the spark. Becoming the embodiment of hate exploded into and took over her mind. The mutilation—really, a perversion—of the natural love bond took the form of psychosis where nightmares break through during wakefulness, becoming reality. It could well be that Eve became her mother, tricked by a satanic figure into getting rid of the "thing" and then laughing at her stupidity.

Aftermath

While Eve was found by the court to be not guilty by reason of insanity and committed to a hospital for the criminally insane, she did not get treatment. Nor did she get understanding. The staff at the hospital didn't want to see the video or my report. To them she was a "baby killer" and therefore dangerous to children in general. They seemed to have no understanding of postpartum psychosis. They kept her indefinitely. What she got was emotional abuse.

Who is crazy? Who is stupid? Who is callous? Who is evil? The know-nothing wave can invade hospitals too.

The Furies are alive and well.

6

Beth

Come with Me

No excellent soul is exempt from a mixture of madness.
—Aristotle

In childbirth grief begins. —Euripides

Children are the anchors that hold a mother to life.
—Euripides

IT WAS AN old, gray courtroom; a very lofty, long, large room, more like a castle hall, with a cathedral feel. There were portraits of ancient, bearded judges hanging on the walls, staring down, disapproving. "Woe be to those who enter these portals."

A young slip of a woman, Beth, stood and started to plead her case. The judge interrupted. "Speak up. I can't hear you."

She wanted full custody of her six-month-old daughter, Angela, and she wanted child support. The child's father, Oscar, had promised to marry her but then abandoned them after Angela was born. He told Beth he'd found a "real woman." He never paid a penny of support. Desperate and angry, Beth threatened to take him to court. That's when she got the legal papers from Oscar's lawyer. He wanted custody for himself. He claimed she was a bad mother.

Beth's world collapsed. Her friends told her not to worry. Oscar was only playing legal games to make her withdraw her child-support demands. When she went to court that first time, Beth didn't think she needed a lawyer. How could anyone question her mothering? She was working two shifts as a rehabilitation nurse to support herself and Angela, and managing to breastfeed. As the baby sucked milk out, Beth felt love and life pouring in—enveloping warmth at her center. Her love for the little one was rapture. Angela was the center of her world, was her whole world.

On the first day in court, Beth's confidence sank when her friend asked how that judge could be involved in her case. He was known to favor men.

Beth grew up in Maine, not far from that very courthouse, but her family lived in a different world than Judge Warlock. Her father, William—or Billy, as he preferred—lost a leg and part of his mind in Vietnam. He stumbled along doing odd jobs between bouts of alcoholism and fighting his demons.

Her mother, Ella, was the foundation stone of the family. A serious, severe woman who always dressed in black, she was very religious. Some said she suffered from religiosity. Ella had two miscarriages, both boys, before Beth was born. She was to be a boy too. They got Beth instead. Mother became depressed, imagined all sorts of things. For a while, she was convinced that she gave birth to a boy. Finally, Mother figured having a girl was God's will.

Ella had been devout before the miscarriages, but after the second, she wrapped herself in the church. She felt the loss of her babies was punishment. She had to do penance. The price included distance from those she loved—and needed. She was scrupulous, was a perfectionist, demanding, impossible to please, a hard woman, and mother.

Billy was soft, warm, affectionate, and adoring of his little girl. He'd sit her on his lap, hug her, and stroke her hair. But she was always aware of his pain. The artificial leg never fit right, and he had to continuously shift. He tried to cover his hurt, but she knew. Beth felt his ache; if only there were some way she could take the hurt away.

As a little girl, Beth sensed there was something wrong with her. She could run and play like the other kids, but she felt ashamed, different. The other kids teased her. "Skinny bones, bent back," they called her, but Mommy and the doctor said she'd outgrow it. She never did feel normal. She felt there was something terribly wrong with her.

When she was nine years old, her mother's doctor said it was a minor degree of a dreadful-sounding medical term. She heard him whisper to Mom, "severe scoliosis." It would cause some disfigurement in appearance. To Beth, it confirmed she was different; not normal, not whole. The doctor dismissed it as a problem that she'd outgrow and be fine. Beth didn't understand and felt confused. She didn't outgrow it. In fact, it got worse.

She was unhappy as far back as she could remember. There were night-mares of monsters, hideous creatures—all deformed—chasing her, trying to devour her. She was helpless, paralyzed; she couldn't run. Afraid to go to sleep, she made up a way to calm herself. She imagined herself lying peacefully in a coffin, hugging her favorite doll to her chest. With that picture in her mind, she sank into darkness and sleep.

When she reached adolescence, she became more sensitive to other "freaks." Beth developed a deep sense of empathy, too deep, too empathic—she felt others' pain. She turned to saving the rejects, the poor, and the helpless.

Animals became her thing. They'd always had cats. Billy liked to bring home some emaciated, droopy specimen he'd rescued. As a young girl, she'd volunteered at the local pound. She loved the saving and healing part but had to steel herself against helping put down the ones that needed death to escape their pain. Her life course was set: help disabled people and animals.

Beth was shy and smart, and she thrived in school. She became a nurse and then a nurse practitioner in a hospital rehabilitation unit.

When she started work there and was able to have her own place to live, she was also able to have her own pet. She ran to the pound and found Kitty. The bonding was immediate. She was surprised at the upwelling of love she felt; Kitty became her baby. But one day, Beth heard the screech of brakes outside, and she knew Kitty was gone. She threw herself into her work.

Beth loved her work with disabled vets. That's how she'd met Oscar. He'd been wounded in the first Iraq War. She thought he was handsome, but most important, he seemed interested in her. She was flattered, seduced that a man found her attractive. She felt he was a kindred spirit because they shared something deep. Both had something wrong: he limped; she had grave doubts about her looks. She was skeletal and small breasted. Friends told her she'd never find a man.

Oscar called. A few months later, there was a miracle. Beth was pregnant. Oscar wanted her to get an abortion, but, how could she? That little life growing inside her was real—made her a real woman. She was a whole woman. Then he promised to marry her if she got an abortion. She couldn't do that. He asked her to move in with him. He said they'd marry later. As the pregnancy wore on, he became more and more abusive. He threw at her what she'd entrusted to him, her feelings about herself. He called her a freak, made fun of her, shoved her, punched her, and one day threw her up against a wall. When she tried to get away, he pushed her down a flight of stairs. Her fear was for the baby inside, and she left.

The custody case dragged on. Then suddenly, she got a notice that the judge had reached a conclusion. Beth went to court. Her heart raced, and her stomach cramped. The judge spoke. He was awarding joint custody, with time and residence split between mother and father. He added that because Oscar suffered from war wounds, Beth was responsible for transporting the baby to and from the father and that he had the option to change the schedule depending on his doctor appointments or the condition of his wound. The question of child support would be decided at some future time.

Beth felt a punch in her stomach, the breath pulled out of her lungs. She was light headed, dizzy, and the room was spinning. She realized that the judge's arrangement would cut off her breastfeeding.

Beth gathered herself and spoke up. She reminded the judge that she was breastfeeding the baby. That would not be possible now under his proposed schedule. Judge Warlock paused, surprised at being questioned, and then with a hint of a sneer pronounced, "Breastfeeding? Young lady, my wife raised four children without breastfeeding. Good enough for her and ours, good enough for you."

Beth was stunned. The room turned dark, and she swore she saw the portraits come alive. Hostile laser beams were coming out of their eyes, straight at her middle.

She had to get out. Her friend, Grace, tried to calm her down. Beth felt heavy and empty at the same time. Her mind was racing; scary thoughts sprang up. The judge and Oscar were working together to take Angela away from her. They could be part of a plot to kidnap children. Oscar could take Angela where Beth could never find her. She felt an overwhelming wave of exhaustion—a desperate sense of hopelessness, helplessness, and dread; a pull of death burst into awareness. It frightened her. She told Grace.

"Let's get you some help," said her friend.

Father John was white haired, steely eyed, and stone faced. Beth told him everything and how she was now scared she might kill herself if she lost Angela. He listened and didn't say anything.

There was a long silence, and then he said, "You have evil inside. There is evil there. Let us pray."

Beth was dazed, damned, devastated—broken. For sure, she would lose Angela. She sank into blackness, emptiness, and despair. She stopped eating; sleep was impossible. In the night, she would tremble and jump out of bed at the slightest noise. She began hearing things. Were there people moving around? Someone coming to take Angela? Were they following her around during the day too, spying and tapping her phone? She'd become drenched, heart and mind racing, terror haunting her.

Death was beckoning, sucking her in. She struggled against the black hole.

The telephone rang. It was Grace. "How you doing? We miss you at work. Something wrong? How'd it go with Father John?"

Beth was hysterical, sobbing, and could hardly get the words out. Grace screamed, "Just don't do anything! I'll be right over!" Grace called the police before jumping in her car. Maybe they could get there sooner.

Beth heard a siren. It was electric—shot into her brain. "Coming—Police are coming to take my Angela. I can't—can't leave my baby. Can't abandon her, my baby, my life, her life. Can't live without her. Can't live without me. Can't abandon her. Come with me. Be together in death—always. No time—the bridge is close."

She cradled Angela in one arm, hugged her close, felt the warmth, the beating heart—and jumped.

Beth awoke in a hospital room. The doctor explained that Angela was dead. Someone saw her jump. She was found still clutching her baby. Beth was being charged with first-degree murder.

Friends consulted experts and got her a respected criminal lawyer. He told them right away, "This is crazy—this was a suicide attempt, not a homicide."

examined Beth in prison. She was deeply depressed, suicidal, and delusional. She asked me to look out the window of the examining room. "See those butterflies? That's Angela coming to visit. See how pretty and happy they are? I'm going to join them."

I asked her if the doctors at the prison saw her, and if she'd told them about her wish for death. She told me the medical staff called her "baby killer." Their way of treating her was to dress her in a paper smock, shackle her to her bed, and take away her Bible. The inmates also called her "baby killer." They avoided her, wouldn't touch her, fearing contamination.

Fortunately, she had good lawyers. They were aghast at the way she was being treated. They went to the warden, and things changed. An experienced, compassionate pastor began to visit.

As the other inmates began to know her, they too changed, accepted her, and were supportive.

My conclusion was that Beth was a young woman at high risk for depression, even before her baby was born. Self-esteem issues stemming back to childhood and tenuous bonding with her mother, with a major theme of doubts and confusion about identity, of being a woman, made her vulnerable and at risk to develop post-partum mental illness. The accusations of her being a "bad mother" struck a sensitive chord, of being a bad, defective woman. In that setting and the cold, degrading attitude of the judge, a full-blown postpartum psychosis with paranoid delusions overwhelmed her.

Her baby was her identity. The prospect of losing her meant the death of them both. In her psychosis, the only way they could be together was in death. Suicide was her motive. From a legal perspective, she fit the definition of insanity.

To make sure, I asked for a second opinion from another highly respected forensic psychiatrist. He did not see my report, and we did not communicate. Our conclusions basically agreed.

There was an excellent case for not guilty by reason of insanity. Beth's lawyers were experienced. They said the judge in this case was fair and compassionate. They thought it might be in Beth's best interests to rely on his mercy, rather than plead insanity and go to trial. They were right. He read the doctors' reports and whatever other information was available. Beth was sentenced to time served, about eight months.

I still worry about her.

Motherhood is not a mold that fits all women. There are different meanings, depending on the individual and her unique life experience. It cannot be understood in isolation. The nature of the woman's relationships, her experiences as a female, can nourish or poison the whole process.

Beth was born into her mother's depression. She was supposed to be a boy, but more importantly, Ella had two miscarriages before Beth. Miscarriages tend to be overlooked and deemed insignificant, but a miscarriage is not only the loss of a child—the loss of dreams, but part of the self too. It can be experienced as a sense of vague personal failure and guilt that is not open to rational explanation. "My body, I, somehow failed my child."

There is a mind-body reaction to loss of greater or lesser degree, again depending on life's experiences and some yet-to-be-determined biological dispositions. A way of defining depression is the bio-psycho-social reaction to loss. It affects the whole person.

Children born to depressed mothers have a greater risk for depression because of its interference with bonding. Attachment between mother and new born is adversely affected by hormonal dysregulation, interpersonal withdrawal, decrease in energy, sense of failure, and other emotional issues are just some of the factors. As an example, Ella's depression wrapped her in guilt and religiosity that disabled her mothering. Their early relationship can best be described as an emotional abandonment. It laid the foundation for basic starvation of Beth's self-esteem. Her lack of confidence came to include the very structure of her body and strongly darkened her sense of value as a woman. Abandonment in any form is the emotional equivalent of death. It is connected with dying. This may be connected with Beth's fantasies of lying in a coffin, hugging her doll to put herself to sleep.

Beth's relationship with her father helped and nourished her sense of empathy—perhaps overfed that ordinarily healthy quality. But empathy can foster pain too, as it becomes a means of comforting others. Taking in others' pain can go too far. Empathy, in that sense, is a double-edged sword.

Beth's self-esteem was fragile. She did not have a firm sense of her womanhood at all or of her value as a person. For her, pregnancy meant she was whole. She was a person, a female person of value. Angela became her; she became Angela, a biological and psychological melding. They were one.

That she was a very bright, sensitive, caring, skilled person didn't seem to count. That the only path to value was proving she was a biological female through bearing a child also reflects a deep cultural bias. She also had the misfortune to run into a judge grounded in medieval misogyny. His action ripped her baby from her breast and ripped her apart.

This is one example of how a unique life history sensitizes a woman to pregnancy. Its meaning to her does not fit the popular mold and greatly increases the development of a related mental illness. This is akin to re-experiencing a past trigger of PTSD much later after the initial episode. There is a hidden vulnerability that can be understood only by a careful, detailed life history. This emphasizes the importance of the psychological complexity in a woman's life.

7

Crystal

I COULD NOT examine Crystal. This is a case of a record review. There was no criminal trial and therefore no trial records. I did receive some psychiatric records, and I filled in the gaps based on my experience. The facts of her life were fairly consistently reported by the newspapers.

Nightmares started during her last pregnancy: God telling her that Jacob, her husband, was Satan. Jacob would be angry if she told him, but he'd ordered her to tell him all her thoughts. Thoughts of cutting her wrists flashed through her mind. She had to report that to Jacob. He said there was an evil spirit inside her, and only pain and prayer would cleanse her. Jacob made her kneel for hours on cracked nutshells with her hands tied in front of her, clasping his Bible, repeating, "Satan leave me."

The pregnancy was hard, like the others. She was sick in her stomach most of the time, sleepless, with no appetite, and she actually lost weight. Depressed? No, she was just irritable and afraid she'd get pulled into blackness and death like the other times. This was the third pregnancy in the five years she and Jacob had been married. She got confused and tried to kill herself after each. She was hospitalized briefly each time. Jacob said if they prayed especially hard that wouldn't happen. She hadn't prayed hard enough before. She worried about Jacob—so quiet, so serious, and so good.

The birth this time wasn't too bad, but when the baby was three months old, the nightmares changed. She'd wake up shaking, sweat drenched, and confused. Jacob was Satan telling her to kill herself and the baby. She heard noises while awake, sounds like whispering. The whispering turned into God's voice, commanding. Jacob was Satan—he must die. She had to kill him. Then she was to punish herself by entering the flames of hell.

Crystal woke about 3:00 a.m. She was awake but in the nightmare. It was real. Jacob was snoring next to her. She found herself in the kitchen and grabbed a butcher knife. Back to their bedroom she went, hearing the loud voice of God, thundering, "Kill him." She stabbed him over and over until he lay motionless.

"Now you!"

She raised the knife, and plunged it through her heart.

Crystal was adopted at birth by a woman, Beverly, whose seven-year-old daughter, Lucy, had drowned two years previously in their swimming pool. Beverly had already suffered two miscarriages before Lucy was born. After the drowning, she felt guilty and empty and sank into a black depression. Her husband, Kyle, suggested she get professional help, but friends told her the surest solution was to adopt quickly.

Crystal was not magical. She made Beverly feel worse by her very presence, a constant reminder of emptiness, guilt, and a longing to reunite with Lucy. She tried to love Crystal but just couldn't muster the energy, just couldn't connect.

Crystal sensed her mother's sadness—and distance. She tried to make Mom happy. She was very, very good, quiet, made no demands, and was obedient to a fault. Nothing worked.

At about five years old, Crystal's stomach pains began. She couldn't eat; she lost weight and became even quieter. The pediatrician said it was a phase. Beverly tried to enroll her in school, but Crystal balked. She just couldn't go. Sick every morning, she couldn't leave home, couldn't leave Mom. When she was at school, she became very nervous, afraid something might happen to Mom. The school's child psychiatrist said it was separation anxiety—and it was time to tell Crystal about the adoption.

It was a silent disaster—a muffled explosion—no questions—blank—gone. No one noted or asked.

As Crystal approached her seventh birthday, Beverly found herself thinking of her Lucy more and more. She told Crystal, "If only you could be Lucy." Then, a week before Crystal's birthday, Beverly impulsively cut her wrists in front of Crystal. The girl hugged her mom but was pushed away. "Let me die."

Shocked, numb, blank, and drained, Crystal turned mute, unreachable. Doctors and family didn't try very hard. No one really asked. For a child to witness parental suicide is a predictor of possible future suicide in one way or another.

Father took over. He'd been pushed out of orbit by Mom but now stepped up and in. Crystal lived with him and Gramps. They were tough, hardworking, steady men who showed their feelings with acts of love, not words. The family trio bonded. Kyle hugged his stone-like daughter. He stroked her hair and whispered that it was not her fault. Gramps sang lullabies, cried as he kissed her cheek. Gradually, she seemed to awaken, soften, to respond, or at least to go through the motions.

Crystal avoided school as much as she could. There were the beginnings of "explosive headaches," which meant more and more doctor visits. The medical tests were negative. No one asked. The doctors did not know her life history.

Periods started at thirteen. The nurse at school had to explain, told her now she could become a mother. The headaches began to fade, but strange stomach and joint pains became so bad, she was given painkillers to help her tolerate school. The stomachaches were passed off as period problems. She took an overdose of narcotics. She wanted only to get rid of the pain.

Crystal was discharged from the hospital after three days, and the social worker who suspected that the overdose was a suicide attempt suggested counseling. The counselor was stumped, but when she learned Crystal was adopted, she said she'd help locate her "real" mom. The counselor didn't ask about the past. There was no real personal history.

Crystal learned to put on a smile; no problems. She was a slim, blond teen beginning to fill out and become attractive. The boys swirled around her. School was a downer, but friends and boys filled her life. The pains faded but never disappeared. There were the occasional headaches that she could only describe as "explosions."

Crystal lost weight. The doctors said it was anorexia and were concerned about the blackouts, blurred vision, nausea, vomiting, diarrhea, and sleeplessness. The headaches returned. She began to lose her balance. She told the doctor she felt like she'd explode. He put her on Xanax. That seemed to make her feel better but subdued. Still there was no history.

At seventeen, she met Raymond, who said he loved her. She stopped the meds on her own and dropped out of school, fastening herself to Ray. She couldn't stand being alone. He was a boy in constant motion, party to party, flirting with every skirt in sight. She was jealous, afraid to say; afraid she'd drive him away. She'd do anything to please him, and she tried to be the fun-loving doll she thought he wanted. From a quiet, reserved introvert, Crystal became hyperactive, always talking, going on and on about nothing. She was running.

A perfect storm was brewing. Crystal became pregnant. Raymond disappeared. During her fourth month, she miscarried. She thought she'd be relieved—she didn't want the baby anyway—but she felt bad, sick, listless. Her father, Kyle, became ill. Crystal forced herself up and struggled to take care of him.

The social worker unearthed her "real mother," who lived in the next town. Crystal called, hoping for some connection. She got slapped down, told never to contact this woman again. The hoped-for reunion was a failure. Wounded, rejected, and abandoned again, she was sliding downward. Panic attacks started. Her doctors were puzzled. They considered her hysterical and referred her to a psychologist, who told her right off not to talk about "negatives—think positives." Still, no one asked.

The next year, the clouds gathered. The storm was beginning to swell. Kyle died suddenly of a heart attack. Gramps was devastated and had a stroke. He too died shortly afterward.

Crystal was numb, dumb, a zombie. Doctors said it was a stress reaction, that she was bipolar, and in denial. They recommended hospitalization, but she refused. They started Prozac and Xanax. Still very depressed, she tried to put an end to her suffering by overdosing, was hospitalized briefly, said she was fine, was discharged, and attempted suicide. She was committed to a state hospital with a diagnosis of "NP" problem. There was no indication that anyone had any idea of what was going on. No one asked.

She did have a few friends who thought they'd help by bringing her to a new church in town, an evangelical congregation with a reputation for miracles. That's what she needed. At the first church gathering, she met Jacob. He also needed a miracle.

Jacob told Crystal he was recently "born again" following his wife's suicide. She'd left him after he'd told her about the nightmares he'd had about her attacking him while he slept. He said her suicide proved she had Satan inside her, and maybe his nightmares were true.

Jacob appeared strong. He also appeared to be the type of personality who can provoke madness. (Sullivan's book on Schizophrenia. Chapter: On Driving Someone Crazy). He was described as a rock, absolutely in control of himself. His beliefs mirrored those of the new church. All spirituality flowed directly from the actual words of the Bible as interpreted by their church and himself.

Crystal was mesmerized, enthralled, and they were married. Jacob believed it was his duty to control Crystal absolutely, to keep her pure in body and soul. That meant her very thinking. His rules included a daily diary of her thoughts, feelings, and actions, including trips to the toilet and the results. At the end of every day, he would go over the diary in detail, correcting transgressions, including the thoughts that Crystal said were unintentional, even alien to her. She could not stop her thoughts about death, which Jacob said was Satan trying to take over.

Another rule was sex daily with no contraception. The Bible replaced medication. The babies followed.

After the first, she seemed fine to Jacob, but she tried to hang herself and was committed to a state hospital again. She saw a psychiatrist, who put her back on medication. Then another baby came, another suicide attempt, and another emergency hospitalization. She stabilized after starting Depakote and was discharged. There was no discussion of the risks of future pregnancies.

After another pregnancy, she stopped seeing the psychiatrist and taking any medication.

Crystal was born on the edge of a black hole. She was sucked deeper and deeper inside until life burned out.

Abandoned by her birth mother, she was adopted by a woman in the midst of a powerful grief that pulled her to reunite with her dead daughter. The drive to reunite with a dead loved one is a bright-red flag for suicide. No one noticed or knew.

Then tragedy multiplied. On the anniversary of the death Beverly's daughter, she committed suicide in front of Crystal by cutting her wrists. Crystal was stamped with suicide one way or another.

No one asked. No one noticed. No one knew—and the seven-year-old girl received no help. At a minimum, letting her know that someone understood her pain could have been helpful, and better yet, encouraged her to talk about her feelings. To try to put them into words is the beginning of healing. Frozen grief—that is, unspoken grief—leads to madness, at best depression, but possibly suicide or murder-suicide.

Instead, her grief depression came out as a variety of physical symptoms, from wandering pains to "explosive headaches." No one asked. She basically was treated as a "hysterical" girl, which devalues and dismisses her. No one looked. No one listened. No one cared.

Later, a series of mental-health services saw her after suicide attempts, but that history is a classic example of the deterioration of our mental-health system into turnstile bandages for lethal conditions. Our helping system remained blind, deaf, and dumb.

This sinking girl grabbed what she thought was a strong lifeline. For Crystal, to become a mother was to enter the portal of death. The internal mix of agony upon agony, unspoken griefs, finally exploded in what was truly madness.

The diagnosis is postpartum psychosis in a mixed mental disease with chronic depressions, psychosomatic equivalents, previous postpartum depressive disorders, possible bipolar disease, and a complicated posttraumatic stress disorder.

8

Agnes

SHE LOOKED AWFUL. If she were white, I would guess Auschwitz or Dachau. No, it was Hartford's North End—and she was coal black. Thirty-two years old, she was charged with murdering her two-year-old daughter and four-year-old son. The neighbors complained about the smell. The police found the two little dead bodies.

Momma was shrouded in bed. She was out cold, foul fumes blowing over white-coated tongue and lips. She was skeletal. The police could hardly feel a pulse. They thought drug overdose and rushed her to the hospital. It was not drugs; it was starvation. She was almost dead.

The medical examiner said the children died of malnutrition. Agnes was charged with neglect, putting her minor children at risk, child abuse, and murder.

Her husband had abandoned her after her youngest was born. Her mother moved in to help take care of the children, allowing Agnes to return to work.

A year later, she came home to find her mother dead in the bathtub, covered in blood with her wrists slit. The children—bloody too—were huddled in the corner. They'd been hugging Granma. No one saw Agnes after the funeral. She disappeared. She'd sunk into herself, disappeared to the outside world. Hopeless, helpless, empty, Agnes gave up living. She made her bed a grave. Her room became the family tomb.

When I interviewed her in jail, I asked about her feelings after finding her mother dead in the bathtub with her wrists sliced. She was blank. "Were you depressed?"

"I've heard that word—people at the jail said—what's it mean? —depressed? Mom's gone. That's all."

The prosecutor asked the same question. He turned to psychiatry for the answer, not to the forensic psychiatrist. He went to the DSM (Diagnostic and Statistical Manual of Mental Disorders), which he cited as the authoritative text of psychiatry, the "psychiatric bible" he called it. The DSM said grief cannot be associated with major depression and indeed suggested that grief somehow protects against depression. Depression, therefore, was not the mental illness claimed to account for "legal insanity." Since her youngest was now two years old, he decided it was far beyond the time limits specified in the DSM for postpartum psychosis. She was found guilty.

Agnes was a black woman, found unconscious, wrapped in sheets in bed, and lying in her own feces. Despite no signs of drugs or paraphernalia, police assumed it was a drug overdose. And the dead children? Did they think she killed them with drugs? They did charge her with murder, but the police attitude is not the biggest problem, although it smacks of racism.

The DSM is particularly weak in dealing with women's issues, or when two or more mental illnesses are involved. Even the most recent version is not clear about either the impact of grief or pregnancy. In Agnes's case, finding her mother dead from suicide with the blood covering her children as well (and after being abandoned by her husband) was disregarded as causative depressive factors because they are not mentioned in the DSM. The understanding of suicide and its impact on survivors is a work in progress. For ages, it has been described like throwing a stone in a pond. Watch the circles spread. But saying that is like blowing in the wind.

The problem is that the Diagnostic and Statistical Manual just does not take into consideration complicated real-life issues. It makes diagnoses in isolation, without regard for connected emotional trauma, with idealized criteria that do not allow for degrees or human variations. It presents time parameters of start of symptoms arbitrarily without regard for human variation. It requires that patients present their diagnosis to the doctor with code symptoms—that is, on a silver platter.

Then we come to Agnes's response to questions about depression.

It is clear she does not know what the word "depression" really means, and she's not alone. It's a term that's bandied about with little understanding. Depression is not simple sadness. The sense of sadness may not even be part of the clinical picture. In my experience, there are many depressed people walking around in denial about their depression and/or other mental-health problems. The masks of mental illness are many. Ask comedians; Robin Williams committed suicide. From stone face to flights into hyperactivity, smiling, alcohol and/or drugs, obsessive work, forced gaiety, the disguises are infinite. All those unexpected suicides or varieties of Russian roulette. Shame and stigma cover a lot of ground, and they muddy the silver platter, if I may mix metaphors.

Another factor that is probably more common than realized is a psychiatric condition called "alexithymia," a very fancy term meaning the person has difficulty or may be entirely unable to think and express his or her emotions in words. The point is, although we rely on words to express feelings, words are a very limited palette, and many of us don't know how to paint.

9

Rachel

RACHEL WAS BROUGHT to juvenile court as a chronic runaway. She'd been running away every few months since she was eleven, two years previously.

Rachel's mother, Ann, had been diagnosed as schizophrenic after the child's birth. She was a senior in college and planned to marry her boyfriend. He broke up with her and broke her when she told him of the pregnancy. Devastated and depressed, she tried to kill herself with booze and pills but woke in the psych ward of the local hospital. Her depression didn't respond to the antidepressants. When she became increasingly noncompliant and told the nurse they were poisoning her and she was hearing voices telling her to kill herself, she was diagnosed as schizophrenic.

Ann's life became a dizzy downward spiral in and out of state hospitals. She'd be hospitalized for a few weeks, put on medication, "stabilized," and discharged. It was a revolving door.

She was usually provided the addresses of a community treatment center and residence, but after discharge, she'd stop taking her meds and end up on the street. Her street was a jungle.

Ann was still fairly attractive and looked for a man to take care of her. Over the years, she had babies by predator males who could easily spot vulnerable prey. Her five child births were followed by suicide attempts. But before she attempted to kill herself, the babies were left on church doorsteps or at an emergency-room entrance. Rachel had been placed in foster care since her birth, but Ann somehow kept track of her.

Ann became less and less attractive over the years and had trouble snaring males. She managed to take Rachel out of foster care, live with her, and take her along while she cruised. Eventually she'd take up, and be taken in, by her "boyfriends." Part of the deal was for Mother to hold Rachel down while they raped the child. Rachel would then run away.

This had been going on for two years until a diligent juvenile probation officer did some digging, despite Rachel's usual response of not revealing anything about her mother, only wanting to return to "Mommy." He found gold.

The issue is the human cost of turnstile psychiatric treatment. This is harmful for the patient, but no one seems to realize there is collateral damage. The family of the patient, children especially, are also damaged. There has been a preoccupation with the rights of patients in terms of the meaning of danger to self and others. The danger is defined as "imminent danger," meaning a patient has to literally say she is going to harm herself and/or others. The emergency commitment usually amounts to about three days. A lucidity is reached in the hospital setting, but upon release, they go back to environmental stressors and a return to their mental illness.

Our laws define harm in concrete terms, meaning violence, but even then, not threatened violence but actual physical assault. Emotional abuse is on the books but ill-defined and rarely acknowledged.

For Rachel, every turn of the turnstile meant gang rape, but her mother's rights to be discharged and refuse treatment trumped Rachel's rights.

There is no single source of psychiatric authority. Science just does not work that way. We do our best to define and trace sources of illness. It is difficult and time consuming. The paths of least resistance are a tendency to either/or thinking and the mind-body split. Shorter hospital stays may be beneficial, but not for all. Family is a highly relevant issue in mental illness. Collateral damage is real.

Presently, we seem to pursue the biological basis of mental illness, whether through genetic, structural, or chemical pathways. These are, no doubt, valuable pursuits and must be continued. But mental illness is truly a bio-socio-psychological process. The mind-body split really does get in the way. It obstructs knowing and understanding the person. Conceptualizing mental illness with all its complications is called for— and for heaven's sake, let's leave politics out. Of course, the elephant in the room is cost, and our society seems to prioritize on the basis of what it really values. Mental illness and psychological issues in general are low on the totem pole.

A detailed life story remains a valuable tool, not only in adding to understanding an illness, but it also puts humanity back in context.

What will become of Rachel, Agnes, Beth, and Eve—and any future children?

I have an educated guess as to Rachel's future, based on my experience with countless juvenile-court cases and substance-abuse cases in all age groups.

Rachel will probably end up addicted to one or more opioids, arrested for related problems of one kind or another at best, or the victim of an overdose, accidental or suicidal. If for some reason her life and/or death makes the media, the public, media gurus, and certainly politicians will wring their hands and ask, "Why, oh why?" But no one will have asked about her life, her mother's too-brief hospitalizations, and the consequences of "turnstile medicine and psychiatry."

IO

Stephanie

Falling between the cracks

STEPHANIE HAD ALL the luck. She had everything. Her friends secretly envied her.

Stephanie had perfect parents. Her father, Ed, was tall; good looking, even to ten-year-olds; very rich, they said; and the top golfer at the club. Mom, Beatrice, was beautiful too, with long blond hair, slim and well-dressed—just right. She could have been a famous writer, Steph told them, but she whispered a secret: Mom and Dad were trying to have another baby—maybe a boy, they hoped. Mom was concentrating on that.

Then it happened: Mom was pregnant. Stephanie said it was secret, but she was so happy—a baby brother on the way. She would help Mom, be a mommy's helper—or something like that.

Little Matthew arrived one sunny day. Stephanie couldn't hold it in. He had dark eyes and hair, but they said that would change. Mom let her hold him, a warm, soft bundle. She loved him very much, and she did help. Mom showed her how to change the diapers, feed him from the bottle; she even read stories to him. Stephanie was very happy. She couldn't wait for summer, to take him to the park.

Matthew must have been about four months old when one morning Stephanie heard a scream. "He's not breathing—he's blue—call the doctor—call nine one-one!" Matthew was dead. They called it "crib death." Stephanie was dumbstruck—what did that mean? They tried to explain, but there was no explanation. Were they blaming the crib?

Pastor John said it was no one's fault; God sometimes takes special children early.

Stephanie changed. She had blanks in her thinking, felt restless, and had trouble concentrating. She couldn't read. Math hadn't been a problem, but now she couldn't keep her mind on the numbers. She was irritable with her friends and family. Everything bothered her, and everyone asked her if she was depressed. Did she miss little Matthew? She wasn't sure what they meant by depressed, but she didn't even feel sad—just angry all the time. She didn't think about the baby. Her teachers said she was distractible, and contrary to her usual self-control was more and more impulsive, jumping up and running into the hall, or disrupting the class with inappropriate speeches.

Her parents brought her to her doctor and told him what was going on. He said it probably was a reaction to Matthew's death, but she'd get over it in time—or it might be ADHD and put her on Ritalin. She did calm down, except she got more and more quiet, seeming to be in her own world. Her grades improved, she was able to concentrate, and rather than irritable, she seemed flat. But that was better than all the fighting. Best of all, she got more obedient and well behaved at home.

Trouble started when Stephanie turned fifteen, and all the talk about how hard it was to get into college began. The pressure to get into a "good" college filtered into the Dupont home. She became obsessed with the thought, "Maybe I'll fail—can't do it—never be accepted." She also became obsessive about "little things." Were her pencils sharpened, were her clothes clean enough, did she look good enough? Her body was changing—were her breasts big enough or too big? She began to believe, really believe, she was fat, even though the scale disagreed. The doctors threw phrases like body dysmorphic syndrome and anorexia.

Stephanie began to have trouble thinking; sentences came together, but some seemed to be unrelated to what she was saying. She wasn't confused, but those listening to her were. She believed more and more people were against her; she knew it. They talked about her; she heard strangers saying she was responsible for Matthew's death. She heard the voices talking to each other about her, and her phone was tapped. She got scared when it occurred to her that people could read her mind and know how evil she was. She panicked, told her parents, and saw a psychiatrist who diagnosed schizophrenia. She needed hospitalization.

This started an odyssey with a downward spiral. She went from one hospital to another. She was treated with the current antipsychotics, "stabilized," and discharged after about a week. The first time that happened, she left the hospital with a prescription, tore it up, and went to the park; that meant peace to her.

The predators in the park latched on to her, gang-raped her, and left her bleeding in the gutter. The police brought her home. Her horrified parents brought her back to the hospital and told them she had to be kept and treated longer. She was, but now she was pregnant. She had the baby in the hospital, and a state agency took the child. Stephanie never saw him again.

She was discharged; she tore up the prescription and ran to the park. The same pack of animals took hold of her, raped her, and left her on her parents' doorstep. This time she was committed to the state hospital. They hoped the commitment would mean she would be kept in the hospital, but times had changed. She had another baby and left with a daughter. She carried her baby to the park, where she left her on a path so someone would find her.

The pack found Stephanie, raped her, and left her to die. The police found her and brought her back to the hospital.

This was repeated several times. Luckily, the babies were found—that is, eight were found. The ninth was left under a bench. It rained, it was cold, and no one came to the park; the baby died.

Stephanie was charged with murder. She sits in prison. The pack will miss her.

How did we get the notion that there was no need for long-term hospitalization? There are some misguided souls who equate hospitalization with incarceration or worse. The movie, One Flew over the Cuckoo's Nest, has turned into blanket condemnation of psychiatric hospitals. But hospitals can be places of safety, havens where healing can take place. Where did we get the notion that medication could heal all problems quickly? It's wishful thinking. Why don't we protect the most vulnerable among us?

II

Adela

Who's Crazy?

The tower of Babel never yielded such confusion of tongues, as the chaos of melancholy doth variety of symptoms.
—Robert Burton: Anatomy of Melancholy, Benediction Classics, 2016

I INCLUDE THIS case because it illustrates how difficult the obtaining of information can be when faced with a mentally disturbed, confused, and confusing subject where there is an important witness equally confused and confusing. But in real life, the way a subject communicates is grist for the diagnostic mill. Adela's accounts in the interviews ramble, skip around in time, do not follow a logical order, and do not appear rationally related.

These patterns express what is called thought disorder, usually considered sign of psychosis. I tried to smooth this out to obtain a working understanding for the reader.

As psychiatrist-detective I had to rely later, on treatment with antipsychotic medication along with obtaining a battery of psychological tests which include a section assessing malingering to clarify the diagnosis. With stabilization from the medication she was more coherent.

Adela, was a twenty-six-year-old single woman who lived at home with her parents. Her initial account before medication indicated she gave birth at home to a baby she believed was dead, drove around with the child in her car, and disposed of the body in a Dumpster. Adela had claimed she was unaware of having been pregnant. She was charged with failure to report a fetal death and wrongful disposal of a dead body.

This initial personal account was taken with a grain of salt as there were secondary gain issues involving whether the baby was born alive, in which case she would be charged with first-degree murder. But she initially stated that throughout the pregnancy, she was unaware she was pregnant, there was no obstetrical care, and her parents were apparently unaware as well.

She said when the baby was born, she realized it was dead but kept it for several days, wrapped in a blanket in her car. She drove around with the body, talking to the baby. She said she heard noises and voices, which she believed were coming from the baby. Finally, in order to stop the voices, she put the body in a Dumpster. It was subsequently discovered, along with evidence linked to Adela. The police concluded that the baby was born dead.

Mother

Although mother was not the subject of the evaluation I was able to form some conclusions about her problems and her influence on the mother-daughter relationship. She would start a sentence directed at describing Adela, but in midstride without being aware, she was talking about herself. From her life story, I concluded the mother-daughter relationship was symbiotic, which means they were pathologically interdependent to the point that their sense of identity lacked individuality.

Mother related that her mother died when she was three months old, and believes her father caused her mother's death although she never offered an explanation. She went on to describe her longing to have a daughter because she wanted to know what it was like to grow up with a mother.

Her son was born first and was described as without problems, but over the course of the next ten years she had "a few miscarriages until I finally got "her." In her description of Adela, it was difficult to tell whether she was talking about her daughter or herself, and she'd go off on personalized tangents.

She went on to describe the mother-daughter relationship as "really close because I was without a mother, so Adela meant more—but as she grew she lied. At this point it was clear that Adela represented her mother's mother.

When asked about her husband: "We are opposites. I'm more assertive—make them mind—obey the first time. I was fortunate with my son. He was born with asthma. We are extremely close. I tried the same with Adela, but she's so changeable."

When asked about Adela's current problem with the law she said, "I think she was drinking quite a bit, and her father has alcoholism in his family. She got carried away—with liquor, things—didn't want to hurt us, but hurt us more. I suspect the father of the baby, but don't believe in revenge. She's her own worst enemy. I'd have to take care of this granddaughter thing. She had an abortion a couple of years ago—actually it was a miscarriage. Then, a year ago, she missed a couple of periods but had fibrous tumors and had to have a D&C or hysterectomy. It was a D&C. I get so confused. She and my husband put on weight and take it off. I'd wonder if she was pregnant."

Adela's mother was assertive, aggressive, and domineering, but the relationship was also symbiotic with over-bonding and dominance. She viewed Adela as an extension of herself. "She looks just like my Mom; Mom died six months before Adela was born."

Adela was described as being quiet, different from other children, and extremely dependent on her mother but resistant at the same time. Her mother indicated that she herself didn't see the difference between what Adela did and getting rid of the products of a miscarriage. Anger suffused her description of virtually all family except her son. She projected blame on her husband and was enraged at her own father. She thought of him as robbing her of her mother. Mother's disorganization is also characteristic of a "thought disorder". In other words, thinking does not appear goal directed. This type of confusion is fundamental in schizophrenia, but occurs in degrees and in Angela's mother case not severe enough to cause disability except in relation to her daughter.

The father indicated that he was raised by his grandparents. His mother died when he was eleven months old, but there was an ambiguity and mystery about her death. His grandparents "put it out of their minds," and his father never talked about it either. "I wondered how I was 'hatched.'" He seemed particularly naïve about sex.

Adela was "Daddy's little girl." He seemed to treat Adela as he imagined his mother would have treated him.

When I first examined Adela, she had a clear understanding of her age, address, and telephone number. She had worked for the past three years as a waitress in a small restaurant.

I found her to be immature, inarticulate, depressed, defensive, and restless. She couldn't sit still, looked around the room frequently, was preoccupied with the space behind her, lost her train of thought, and had to be brought back to the subject or she'd go off on a tangent. She claimed virtually total unawareness of emotional problems.

Thinking was distorted with ideas of reference, meaning an over personalization of situations that had no real connection to her. Thinking also had a vague paranoid quality, but without systemized delusions. She rocked back and forth intermittently and seemed to be responding to auditory hallucinations.

She denied being aware of the pregnancy but acknowledged drinking more heavily, upward of a six pack a day during that period.

The psychiatric findings indicated Adela was a highly-disturbed person, suffering from a complex mental illness, including a form of schizophrenia. She functioned on a primitive, profoundly immature level, and was probably symbiotic with her mother.

This was a highly-disturbed family under a conventional façade.

I knew that Adela had to be stabilized and psychologically tested in order to clarify her mental illness. Psychological testing was consistent with schizophrenia.

Treated with an antipsychotic medication, she revealed that she suspected pregnancy at about fourteen weeks and consulted a clinic for testing. The clinic confirmed pregnancy. Adela proceeded with her life as though the pregnancy did not exist. The clinic gave her the option of abortion or having the baby. "I was supposed to get back to them but didn't think about it."

She said the father of the baby was a good friend, but she stopped seeing him when she discovered the pregnancy. She became evasive when pressed further.

Her feelings about the pregnancy were confused: "I don't know—didn't know what to think—do. I was scared—put off finding out definitely—didn't think and didn't give myself time to think. I took up my time working hard, drank a lot, and go to sleep. Just lived with it—that's all."

When asked about her feelings she replied, "Didn't think about it—sometimes I heard my name called. I hear things now too. I wake up hearing sirens. I heard Mom calling me—she fell down some stairs. Voices, 'You shouldn't be doing that.' My mind's a blank—can't concentrate—people talking about me—strangers—in public—everyone looks at me."

She described her mother as "Very generous, very understanding, and persuasive ---I wouldn't trade her. I'm an only daughter. She's always there; she gets things done. With my father, she gets her way—always for the good---for a time, I became very stubborn—had to do things myself. Then found out I should have done it her way—my way I'd end up breaking something. She was understanding."

"Would she punish?" "Yes, but it was always well deserved."

Adela described her father: "I'm very much like him, he always thinks of others first. I'm Daddy's little girl. He's rattlebrained; he forgets easily and gets flustered in emergencies."

She described her older brother "as perfect as a human or brother could be—sensible, quite a thinker, never had a fight, took me everywhere. I'm his pal, his little sister. He's always there. Sometimes I think he's too sensitive, but then I think something's wrong when he's not."

She described herself as very dependent on her parents now but rebellious as a teen. She said she had temper tantrums when she was younger and was "apt to get my way." At the same time, her brother was her ally in manipulating her parents. The brother and parents were described as highly protective. She also described herself as impulsive: "I do things without thinking and that's what got me in this mess."

"Can you tell me what happened?"

What follows is her account which is so disjointed that it was difficult to follow, but that is just one example of her thinking disorder. I was used to that so just let her go on.

That day, "I wasn't feeling well and decided to take a bath. After a while I felt sick in my stomach. I thought there was too much water in the tub so I let some water out. The baby started to come out, I saw the head and remember holding its head so it wouldn't go in the water so it wouldn't hit the tub. I didn't see the face but remember picking up its arm—it was blue—it didn't move, it just dropped---I started to cry---I got out, and sat on floor. That's where the baby was born. I took her to bed with me. I knew she wasn't alive, but. uncovered her, checking to see if she was breathing for a long time. I kept her in my bed, and finally went to sleep---next day I didn't tell anybody---wrapped her up in bedsheets---took her in my car. I was driving around---kept hearing her—kept seeing the arm—crying—my name---had to get rid of the voices—threw the bundle in a Dumpster—that didn't get rid of the voices—kept hearing voices---me calling to my mother--- knew there was a haunting there."

Adela's mental illness illustrates how complex mental illness can be. Although her signs and symptoms add up to schizophrenia on most scales, her mental illness is really just one element in what might be called a family psychosis.

Adela's mother suffered several miscarriages before Adela was born and may have played a role, as well as the early loss of her mother and its consequences, on her disordered mind.

There was so much mental illness here; it's hard to know where to begin. The main point I want to make is the importance of the person's history and including in the evaluation persons close to the subject, especially those who play an important role in the life story. This is psychiatric detective work, which takes time and a lot of digging.

Mental Illness

Mental illness is complicated. There are many subtle yet powerful influences in a unique life history. Medical diagnosis rightly relies on the characteristic course of a disease, but we recognize that the course also is influenced by the vagaries of life. No two persons have the same life experiences, even twins. The course of any disease will depend on the individual's unique biological and social experience. No two cancers are the same. Mental illness is similar. It can lie dormant, develop slowly, and later emerge within a psychological context that strikes a resonant chord. The various presentations can be mind boggling. The psychiatrist has to be a detective.

There are analogous situations in biological medicine, like sensitizing conditions in childhood that can much later surface in adulthood, or particular situations, like travel to areas of infectious risk or living in or working in environmentally risky areas. If only we could accept that child abuse or other emotional trauma can work the same way.

The deepest reason for our psychological blindness is to close our eyes to pain—emotional pain. We all have it or the seeds of it that can sprout when watered by tears.

Emotional pain flows from such circumstances as failure, abandonment, rejection, guilt, shame, and even overflowing empathy when we take in another's agony. At the center of depression is the suffering of losing someone or something of importance. Loss is such a simple word, but the death of a child, beloved parents, spouse, friend, or siblings can cause drowning waves of sorrow. When it comes to multiple losses, loss by suicide, or loss by murder, it may be very difficult to find the words to express the agony. The danger then is walled-off grief.

When grief is bottled up, it can become an abscess or cancer eating away inside, infiltrating the soul, the center of the self in our subconscious minds. The abscess may be silent, but it grows there deep inside, pushing, waiting for release.

Life is a journey—our unique life story. We cannot know what we'll meet down the road, what we will run into, or what will run into us. Life may seem sunny and calm, but a perfect storm can strike, touching and triggering our deepest sensitivity, our vulnerability—piercing an unrecognized abscess.

Examples

The following examples illustrate the diversity of how mental illness is caused, submerged, later triggered, emerges and the variation in presentation.

(1) Anna, a Cambodian refugee, saw her teacher parents ripped from her and sent into darkness never to return. She and her sister were sent to a work camp. The rule was if any inmate appeared slow, complained, or showed any sign of fatigue, they would be put in a circle of other inmates, a hood would be placed over the head, and they would be beaten until dead.

Anna had to watch her sister being bludgeoned to death, and she did not make a sound. The soldiers told her she couldn't. If she did, she would be next. She obeyed. She never voiced it to anyone, not to other family, friends, or even to her husband, and certainly not to anyone in authority. She put it out of her mind—she thought.

Years later, working in a factory, her sleeve got caught in a grinding machine, pulling her into the chewing gears. The shoulder injury was not severe, and the surgeons got an "excellent result," but the pain did not go away. It got worse and worse, becoming agonizing.

As her arm was being pulled into that machine, the image of her sister bludgeoned and the ghosts of her parents who had been severed from her rose from the empty deadness inside, filling Anna with pain.

(2) When the last dirt echoed off Grandpa's coffin, Jason twisted around and ran to his car. It was so sudden, everyone turned and wondered, "What the hell?"

He drove carefully to the highway and then zoomed. When the speedometer hit ninety, he heard the siren and saw the blinking lights of the cruiser. He quickly pulled over, turned off the ignition, opened his door, stepped out, and started walking slowly toward the state trooper who was coming toward him. Their eyes locked.

Jason raised his right arm, pointing toward the officer. His hand held a gun. Officer Leary yelled, "Stop!" Jason said nothing. He just kept walking, step by step, his gun aimed at the officer's heart. Leary pulled out his gun and again said, "Stop." Jason's face was blank. He didn't stop. His finger tightened on the trigger. Leary fired. Jason fell.

Leary bent over Jason. "I thought so. This guy's gun is a fake, a toy, but it sure looks real. Why didn't I shoot to kill? There was just something about him. I know I took a big chance, but there was just something." He spelled it all out in his report: attempted suicide by cop.

Jason was a veteran. He went bloodlust mad when he found his buddy decapitated. He butchered the next village. He massacred a whole family. There was an old man with a little boy on his lap. Their faces seared his brain. They haunted him. Alcohol and cocaine helped some, but not when his grandpa died.

(3) On his eighteenth birthday, that was it. Billy packed his book satchel and went to school as usual. But today he ducked into the boy's room and waited. When the bell rang and he could hear footsteps in the hall, he stepped out and began firing.

Billy's mother died giving birth to him. His father sank into de-pressive rage and alcoholism. He blamed Billy. The boy grew up being called a murderer while being beaten with a leather-coated bicycle chain. He'd be beaten harder if he cried. It was all hidden; no marks outside.

His humanity was beaten out of him.

(4) Joe was tough, a Vietnam veteran, and a highly-decorated state troop-er for twenty-plus years. He thought he'd seen everything. He'd been shot at, shot, rammed by a car, and seen the gore and death of count-less accidents and domestic violence. He was tough, and one of the best at corralling the bad guys.

Then one day he got an emergency call. There was a jumper on a bridge. He grabbed the man's arm, but the jumper twisted, arms tangled, slid; he had him by the wrist, another twist. The jumper was gone. Joe was tough, but he fell apart. It all came back, erupted,

Vietnam. It was not the fear of death, the terror, the explosions, the hidden enemies, or the killing. He was the sole survivor of his unit. He saw all his brothers-in-arms die. He thought he had put all that out of his mind until the moment the jumper was gone. He was unable to save that life too.

Then it all came flooding back, drowning him.

Everyone had said how lucky he was to survive, but he couldn't or wouldn't talk about it, and somehow, he never got to Washington to see the memorial.

(5) The plump, graying grandmother walked into the store, put on a dress, then another over the first, then another over that, and on and on until she could hardly walk. The sales lady standing right there was speechless. Grandmother then waddled out of the store where she was immediately stopped and charged with shoplifting. This was not the first time. This had been going on for years. She was always caught.

When she was ten years old her family was deported to a work camp. On her eleventh birthday, her father took her with him as he sneaked past the guards and over the barbed wire. He took her to the nearby town where there was a clothing store, and told her to wait outside while he broke in and got her a birthday dress. She waited and pretty soon her father appeared with a dress over his arm. The soldiers were waiting too and shot him dead washing her feet and the dress in his blood.

Depending on our unique psychological immune system, that triggering event can open the abscess, releasing an emotional upsurge transformed into symptoms. Unexplained pain and other psychosomatic maladies are examples; but that release of emotions can result in action symptoms. This means acting out the emotions, and if intense enough, explosive actions, the most dramatic of which we read about in the newspapers. Explosions are not always outward and not always loud. Actually, most go silently inward and become a life of quiet and hidden misery. Some end in suicides we read about in an obituary as a "death of unknown cause," and many end up in doctors' offices, seeking explanations and relief for pain of unknown cause.

12

Perspective

Furies to Juries: A Tale of Four Cities

This chapter was published in the online journal ElectrumJanuary2, 2017. I added ed details to flesh it out.

SCIENCE IS THE body of laws of nature, or the seeking of those laws; psychiatry is the science of human nature. Ultimately it is the science of emotional pain, and of paradox that, contrary to nature, can lead us to cause pain to others and ourselves. We humans are capable of acting at odds to our own survival. In fact, we can be quite destructive—self-defeating and self-destructive. We are the only animals to knowingly commit suicide. And we kill singly, in scores, thousands, even millions for seemingly no, little, or for the flimsiest of reasons. We can commit genocide based on ideology, symbol, myth, or less. We carry a savage primitive core.

What is justice? Is it simply retribution—an eye for an eye, with the ultimate exaction being death? And if so, what is the larger purpose of justice? What function do we want it to serve? Aside from the satisfaction of revenge, is there any other benefit? Are there hidden costs? And what, if anything, does psychiatry bring to these questions?

To our courtrooms come mind-boggling barbarity. There are all the variations of human cruelty, depravity, and destructiveness that threaten our fragile fabric of civilization. We rely on justice to maintain that fabric.

As a young doctor, I had been trained in the classic ways of learning the workings of the body separately from mind. Fortunately, during my internship I was exposed to a way of bridging the mind-body divide---more importantly, a way of knowing the person who carries a disease as a path to knowing the disease, and more effectively relieving their suffering.

That was a stepping stone. I was drawn to questions of emotional pain, and why we hurt and kill, destroy ourselves and those we love. That's why I became a psychiatrist and forensic psychiatrist. Pulled out of the hospital into prisons and courtrooms, at the interface of psychiatry and the law, I found myself in a place where our society tries to solve problems in human nature by means of a system called justice. More paradox.

Justice asks for assistance in making intelligent decisions when mental illness is relevant. Intent, motivation, and what makes someone tick is important in sentencing as well as establishing guilt. There is, however, controversy about psychiatry's role in our legal system. For some three hundred years, the controversy has been heated. It comes to a boil when there is a political assassination such as the attempt on President Reagan. I needed to understand the controversy, and our twenty-first-century's role in working with justice. I thought a good place to start was exploring the history of the insanity defense.

The exploration turned into a journey. I traveled much farther than I expected, and took some surprising turns and touched down in unanticipated places. I landed at the birth of our western civilization with the beginning of science in ancient Greece.

I met the midwife of that birth, Thales, who had the revolutionary idea that it was not the gods who controlled the natural world. The seeming chaos of nature, storms, tides, seasons, and the movement of stars was the result of underlying laws of nature. Thales was the first scientist. There were no gods, and mythology was stories made up to explain the unknown.

From the stars to the earth under our feet, the world could only be understood by observation and logical reasoning. Mythology was myth. He taught the scientific method. His realization that natural phenomena can only be understood by observing and reasoning became the road to civilization. At the next stop on that road I met the first political scientist.

A Tale of Four Cities: Athens, Rome, London, and Washington

Our western legal system called democratic justice evolved from the need to tame our savage nature. The earliest civilization relied on revenge justice, an "eye for an eye" in Biblical terms, or in Greece, "to the doer be done." The victim, his or her family, tribe, clan, village, or country did punishment—see Trojan War, Rwanda, Iraq, the history of the Middle East and much of our modern history. It resulted in vendettas and never-ending cycles of violence. Revenge justice, or "wild justice," as Francis Bacon later called it, was tearing apart infant civilized society.

Justice as we know it dates back to the sixth century BCE in Athens. Those dark times needed a law giver, a Moses. They got Moses plus, but on his own, without a god. Solon was a poet, philosopher, soldier, merchant, practical economist, and social critic. He shines out of antiquity. Solon came to power as revolution was knocking on the door. The ruling aristocracy, oligarchs in our terms, were desperate They called on the warrior poet Solon— appointed him chief archon (governor). His mission: put an end to the cycles of retaliatory violence that had plagued Greece for centuries. Athens wanted peace and order. Solon had let the people know his vision of the root cause of social disorder as a kind of human disease—greed, and the cure was real justice. He expressed this through his poetry. It was ancient Facebook at its best. Solon's message should be read by our politicians.

Solon laid the foundation for a democratic justice system. In what can be compared to the creative legislative eruption of Roosevelt's First Hundred Days to meet our Depression's crisis, Solon drafted the first of a series of constitutions that gave birth to democracy. He established a public court system and legal code that brokered a nonviolent social revolution. He converted private revenge into public justice. This system was based on the rule of law and equality before the law. There was redistribution of power, resolution of conflict through public adversarial trials before a presiding judge. Complaints could be brought by non-relatives, opening the development of what today we call attorney advocates. He instituted the right to appeal. Juries of peers were selected by lottery. If this sounds familiar it should. That's where our system comes from.

Religion was separated from the administration of justice for the first time in human history, and thousands of years before Lincoln, Solon abolished debtor slavery. A stated purpose of his constitution was to build a middle class which he saw as central in democracy. His first order was to stop all exports except olive oil. Voting was severed from birthright. He reformed the monetary system, and created a government of executive, legislative, and judicial branches. He encouraged immigration of skilled labor while making a policy that fathers had to teach sons a craft. He did away with the aristocracy's (oligarchs in our terms) reliance on inherited wealth and position. Solon introduced what became central to democracy: the right to trial by a jury of peers and the right to appeal.

He gave power to the landless by opening jury selection, and deliberately made the legal code ambiguous enough to encourage litigation enabling the landless to exert considerable power. He discouraged ostentatious shows of wealth.

Solon harnessed "wild justice," and made it a central part of democracy.

These developments occurred in the context of the birth of science. Solon seized the concept of natural law and applied it to governance. Human nature was being recognized as a part of nature, and had its natural law. As the movement of the stars, storms, tides, and seasons were understood to be the result of underlying laws of nature rather than visitations from gods, so too were the mysteries of behavior, the storms of emotions, and life-cycle seasons understood to be influenced by laws of human nature. This was the beginning of psychology.

Solon incorporated psychology into his legal code. As an example, he made seduction of a married woman a crime, saying it was a corruption of a woman's mind which was worse than the corruption of flesh. Understanding what was in the mind of the accused became a priority. Manslaughter and intentional homicide had been differentiated even under Draco, but intent and motive became more important under Solon. He laid the foundation for our mens rea concept two thousand years before the English discovered it in the classics.

Instead of absolute liability, the law looked to specific, underlying, differentiating, and causative factors. Punishment was proportional to the crime. You could not be hung or imprisoned for stealing a loaf of bread a la Draco. Preventing violence and maintaining public order were stated purposes of law. He was aware of the plight of women; they now could own property, had rights of inheritance, and freed widows from having to marry their husband's brother. He did away with the dowry saying it made women chattel. This was sixth century BCE Athens!

The influence of Athenian democratic justice can be seen every day in every courtroom in our land. We would not have that influence, however, but for the genius of another man coming some one hundred years after Solon.

Aeschylus was poet, philosopher, soldier, and, like Solon, a fighter for democratic justice. Aeschylus's genius lay in drama. He was the creator of tragic drama. He used his art as a weapon in the defense of law, and the peaceful resolution of conflict. During his time, political upheaval threatened to sweep away constitutional reforms. Athens also had its constitutional crisis.

Amid the constitutional crisis of 458 BCE, Aeschylus produced the Oresteia, the greatest tragic drama in human history. Ironically, the play's ending is not tragic. It nourishes hope.

The Oresteia is a window into the evolution of Athenian justice, the principles underlying its law, and the threats inherent in human passions. The play is a plea for democratic justice.

The third play, act in our terms, of the trilogy is a courtroom trial in which the mental state of the defendant is central. It has all the elements of what today we call legal insanity. The staged trial with judge, prosecution, defense counsel, and jury of peers reflected the actual Athenian system established by Solon some one hundred years previously.

The Oresteia immortalized the message of democratic justice. This powerful drama kept alive the idea of humanism in justice: through the hardening and decline of the Roman Empire; through the submersion in the Dark Ages; through the rebirth of the classics in the Renaissance; to the British Isles; and to our courtrooms. The Oresteia became the vital voice of Solon's justice that enabled it to survive.

The Athenian legal system served as a frame of reference for the codification of Roman law. Cicero was a Roman philosopher, statesman, lawyer, orator, and political scientist. He is also said to be a rejected lover of Cleopatra. He had absorbed the Greek legal system while living and researching in Athens. He returned to Rome and transfused the Roman codes with the Athenian humane values. He created the term Humanitas.

Recent translations of some of Cicero's homicide defense cases cite Aeschylus's Oresteia as an example of legal insanity. Athenian law contributed to the evolution of a great and complex Roman legal system. And the Italian scholar and poet, Petrarch, credits the development of the Renaissance in the fourteenth century to the rediscovery of Cicero's writing. Cicero's legacy also contributed to the Enlightenment of the eighteenth century.

Then as Rome deteriorated, civilization sank into the darkness of "the worst of times." Justice seemed to be extinguished by societies ruled by the occult, greed, power, and raw vengeance. The furies rose again and took over justice. Magical thinking and belief in the supernatural buried science. Mysticism, cloaked in religion, drowned awareness of scientific thinking and compassion. Belief in demonology and witchcraft became a wild fire tool of aristocratic politicians and the priestly class. They used fear and malignant scapegoating to exploit the underclass, and fuel a lust for power. Rational understanding was knocked down, comatose.

But justice and science were not dead. They lay dormant, hibernating in those literary treasuries of classical Greece and Rome, stored away in Islamic libraries, and ecclesiastical archives. It has been a slow and fitful reawakening.

Threatened by the Moslem infidel, the Eastern Church in Constantinople transferred the original Greek cultural masterpieces to safety in Rome. These classics, including Cicero's writings, had been presumed lost for a thousand years, but had been hidden away in the bowels of churches. When Rome too was about to be overrun by barbarians, the literary treasures continued their odyssey from east to west, Italy to Ireland, Scotland, to the British Isles, and to the continent, and back to England with William the Conqueror in AD 1066. The foundation was laid for the founding of English Common Law between AD 1160 and 1270.

Slowly English society developed in a more representative direction. An entrenched priestly class and residue from feudalism inhibited growth. But the adversary system, verdict power of the jury, and the concept of equality before the law reemerged from antiquity to see and shed light. With the growth of the adversary system in England the legal profession gained strength and gradually replaced the ecclesiastical jurists.

The last great ecclesiastical jurist, also a classical scholar, was Henry de Bracton, known for his recognition of psychological factors as important in law. He contributed to the slow rebirth of the concept of legal insanity. Author of On the Law of England, he is a link between justice as developed in Athens and Rome and the evolving law in England.

After Bracton, the principle of intent again entered justice. There was more recognition of "unsound mind" rather than witchcraft, and by the fourteenth century complete madness was a defense. By the sixteenth century the concept of non- compos mentis, legal insanity, was further understood with the recognition that there could be lucid intervals, an understanding that tends to get lost in our current courtrooms. Mens rea, guilty mind, or the awareness that one's act is criminal, was made a necessary element if an act was to be considered a crime. Humanistic ideals were reborn with justice at the center.

During the Enlightenment universities were founded and fed social institutions with a rediscovered appreciation for scientific curiosity. There was a return to seeking rational explanations for natural phenomena—back to those first Greek natural philosophers. Rediscovering the wheel.

This was the beginning of the struggle against demonology and its modern derivative "evil." In that struggle, the ancient Greek idea of a rational approach to the understanding of nature, human nature, and society has been opposed by residua of our medieval legacy. The battleground has often been our courts where, since Solon's and Aeschylus's time, the nature of humankind is debated.

The warriors for rationality and their battleground cases resound through modern history. Johan Weyer confronted the law in AD 1572 maintaining that confessions of witches were the result of mental illness. His views were dismissed as merely those of a physician. Mental illness was demonized, driving a wedge between psychiatry and the law that has not been completely bridged to this day. Yet the English jurists Coke, Hale, and Francis Bacon were responsive to psychological developments, which they attempted to integrate with law.

Edward Coke was chief justice during Victorian times. Equality before the law, meaning even the king was subject too, was established. Of course, no credit was given to Homer who raised the idea when he said that even Zeus had to abide by a natural moral law.

Thomas Jefferson and John Adams referenced Coke as they wrote our Constitution. Adams cited Solon in *The Political Writings of John Adams*, (Carey, Regnery Publishing.)

Although English law continued to trail scientific growth, during the eighteenth and nineteenth centuries advance in psychiatric knowledge began to infiltrate. Scotland produced two great minds, one legal and the other psychiatric. Thomas Erskine had defended Thomas Paine and was considered England's leading trial lawyer. Alexander Crichton (1763–1856) authored *An Inquiry into the Nature and Origin of Mental Derangement*.

His work focused on the influence of emotions on thinking processes. He contributed to the development of modern psychiatry. Crichton was the first to describe in accurate clinical detail what today we call Attention Deficit Hyperactivity Disorder (ADHD), long before it resurfaced in medical literature. And more than a hundred years before Freud, he explained certain speech disorders by the psychological concept of word association—the underlying meanings attached to word processes. He pointed out that Aristotle first described associative thinking. That was about two thousand years before Freud.

When in 1800 James Hatfield attempted to assassinate George III, Erskine was called to defend him. He called Crichton as his expert. Law and psychiatry were joined. They took the law into the complexities of mental illness and the relevance of delusions in legal insanity.

Forensic psychiatry was germinating, nurtured by developments in the psychological and neurosciences. William Cullen, a pathologist, published his study of insanity, and his students, Benjamin Rush in America and Pinel in

France, extended his influence. Benjamin Rush, in addition to being one of the founders of our country, was instrumental in the humane treatment of the mentally ill.

Pinel, Pritchard, Esquirol, and Isaac Ray were raising issues of the forensic implications of emotions. They focused on how intense emotional states can impair the ability to control behavior. But the English courts were still grappling with the issues of mental illness, reluctant to give up old notions of global dysfunction as the legal definition of mental illness in criminal cases.

The last 175 years have been a roller coaster. In 1838 the American psychiatrist, Isaac Ray, in *A Treatise on the Medical Jurisprudence of Insanity* sifted and synthesized the developing psychiatry and applied it to an understanding of criminal behavior. Ray took psychiatry into more complex and less readily knowable areas of the mind than the Hadfield case considered. His work led to the conceptualization of what he called "irresistible impulse," of how distorted, diseased emotions can overwhelm rational thinking, sometimes in sudden explosive acts, but also over time with a gradual, losing struggle to keep from doing what the rational mind abhors. He emphasized that "the affective (emotional) as well as the intellectual" faculties are subject to derangement." In other words, insanity can mean more than impairment of "knowing" right from wrong. A mentally ill person can know an act is legally and morally wrong, but be unable to stop himself/herself from doing it.

He also considered the complex problem of lucid intervals, simulated insanity, malingering, concealed insanity, suicide, and the difficulty for juries in remaining objective about heinous crimes. He laid this out for all to read.

It reverberated in 1843 at the trial of Daniel McNaughton, a paranoid schizophrenic, who had killed a British aide to the prime minister in an assassination attempt. The English chief justice had recently read Ray's work on the role of delusions. He found McNaughton was not guilty by reason of insanity. The judge cited McNaughton's paranoid delusions causing his homicidal act, and his inability to control his behavior. The acquittal struck a raw nerve in society, fueling fear and threatening the sense of social order. It set in motion waves of opposition to the insanity defense and to psychiatry. Those waves still lap our shores.

The media storm moved parliament and the queen to overturn the judge's decision resulting in what has come to be known as "The McNaughton Rules" stating that the test for legal insanity is "knowing an act is wrong." The role of emotional illness and "irresistible impulse" be damned. This has come down to us as the basic principle. It represents a step back. Significantly, even though more modern justice intellectually recognizes "the inability to conform conduct to the law," in actual practice McNaughton rules.

The struggle has been to bring scientific understanding of the mind into legal deliberations. But the critics of moral law have interpreted science for their own agenda. Following the Civil War, the theory of social Darwinism exerted undue influence on many legal scholars. The result was to diminish humanism, compassion, and psychology. Oliver Wendell Holmes, Jr. went so far as to suggest morality has no place in law, and that legal adjudication that includes morality has no constitutional basis. It was impossible for him to know that social Darwinism was to become the tool of fascism.

Justice Holmes in 1881 in The Common Law 46 wrote, "It may be said, not only that the law does, but that it ought to make the gratification of revenge an object. The first requirement of a solid body of law is that it should correspond with the actual feelings and demands of the community, whether right or wrong. If people would gratify the passion of revenge outside of the law, if the law did not help them, the law has no choice but to satisfy the craving itself, and thus avoid the greater evil of private retribution." This is back to Draco.

The last three hundred years have been a turbulent struggle to solve this very old and complex problem---passion for revenge.

The circle completes, from Athens, to Rome, to London, to Washington. But this leaves us in 2017, 2400 years from Solon, 440 years from Johan Weyer and 175 years from Isaac Ray, still emerging from the Dark Ages, technologically enlightened, but socially and legally regressed with justice partially stuck in medieval myths and politics, and only partly tamed.

*"At his best, man is the noblest of all animals: separated from law and justice he is the worst---***Aristotle**

Bibliography

Ezra Griffith, M.**D.,** Aleksandra Stankovic, MA., and Madeline Baranoski, PhD., Conceptualizing The Forensic Psychiatric Report as Performative Narrative, J Am Academy Psychiatry Law, 38:1:32-42(March 2010)

Friedman, Susan. M.D. Horowitz, Sarah PhD. and Resnick, Philip, M.D. *Child Murders by Mothers: A Critical Analysis of the Current State of Knowledge and a Research Agenda*, online American Journal of Psychiatry, Sept. 01, 2005

Connell, Michele. "The Postpartum Psychosis Defense and Feminism: More or Less Justice for Women." *Case Western Law Review* 53, no. 1 (2002): 143–53.

Resnick, Philip and Hatters-Friedman, Susan, *Infanticide: Psychosocial and Legal Perspectives on Mothers Who Kill,* Psychiatric Services, published online August 01, 2003

Friedman, Susan, M.D. and Resnick, Philip, M.D. *Child Murder by Mothers: patterns and prevention,* World Psychiatry 2007 Oct. 6)3): 137-141

D'Orban, P. T. "Women Who Kill Their Children." *British Journal of Psychiatry* 134, no. 6 (1979): 560–71.

Greenblatt, Steven, *The Swerve, How the World Became Modern*, W.W. Norton & Company, New York, 2011

Engel, George. *Psychological Development in Health and Disease.* Philadelphia: Saunders Publishing, 1962.

Ewing, Charles Patrick. *Insanity, Murder, Madness, and the Law.* Oxford: Oxford University Press, 2008.

Fingarette, Herbert. *The Meaning of Criminal Insanity.* Berkeley: The University of California Press, 1972.

American Psychiatric Association. *Diagnostic and Statistical Manual of Mental Disorders.* 4th ed. Arlington, VA: Author, 1994.

———. *Diagnostic and Statistical Manual of Mental Disorders.* 5th ed. Arlington, VA: Author, 2013.

Aristotle. *The Athenian Constitution.* Translated by P. J. Rhodes. London: Penguin Classics, 1984.

Aristotle. *Athenian Constitution.* Translated by H. Rackham. Cambridge, MA: Harvard University Library, Loeb Classical Library, 1992.

Biggs, John, Jr. *The Guilty Mind.* New York: Harcourt, Brace & Co., 1955.

Burrows, Edwin G., and Mike Wallace. *Gotham: A History of New York City to 1898.* Oxford: Oxford University Press, 1998.

Burton, Robert. *The Anatomy of Melancholy.* Oxford: Benediction Classics, 2016.

Carey, Christopher. *Trials from Classical Athens.* London: Routledge, 1997.

Carey, George, ed. *The Political Writings of John Adams.* Washington, DC: Regnery Publishing, 2000.

Aeschylus. *The Oresteia*. Translated by Robert Fagles. New York: Bantam Books, 1977.

Cicero. *Murder Trials*. London: Penguin Classics, 1990.

Cohen, David. *Law Violence, and Community in Classical Athens*. Cambridge: Cambridge University Press, 1997.

Crichton, Alexander. *An Inquiry into the Nature and Origin of Mental Derangement, Volumes 1 and 2*. London, 1798, ECCO Print Editions.

Ehrenberg, Victor. *From Solon to Socrates*. London: Routledge, 1996.

Freeman, Kathleen. *Trials from the Athenian Law Courts*. New York: The Notable Trials Library, 1995.

Goldstein, Abraham S. *The Insanity Defense*. New Haven, CT: Yale University Press, 1967.

Hermann, Donald H. J. *The Insanity Defense*. Springfield, IL: Charles C. Thomas, 1983.

Homer. *The Iliad*. Translated by Robert Fagles. Introduction and notes by Bernard Knox. London: Penguin Classics, 1991.

Hunter, R., and I. Macalpine. *Three Hundred Years of Psychiatry 1535–1860*. New York: Carlisle Publishing, 1982.

Kendler, Kenneth S. "The Phenomenology of Major Depression and Representativeness and Nature of DSM Criteria." *The American Journal of Psychiatry* 173 (2016): 771–80.

Kitto, H. D. *The Greeks*. Harmondsworth, Eng.: Penguin Books, 1991.

Lewis, John. *Solon The Thinker*. London: Duckworth, 2006.

Maeder, Thomas. *Crime and Madness*. New York: Harper and Row, 1985.

Manchester, William. *A World Lit Only by Fire*. New York: Back Bay Books, 1993.

Mehl-Madrona, Lewis. *Healing the Mind Through the Power of Story*. Rochester, VT: Bear and Company, 2010.

Oshinsky, David. *Bellevue, Three Hundred Years of Medicine and Mayhem in America's Most Storied Hospital*. New York: Doubleday, 2016.

Parkes, Colin Murray. *Bereavement, Studies of Grief in Adult Life*. Madison, CT: International University Press, 1979.

Perlin, Michael L. *The Jurisprudence of the Insanity Defense*. Durham, NC: Academic Press, 1994.

Plutarch. *The Rise and Fall of Athens: Nine Greek Lives*. Harmondsworth, Eng.: Penguin Books, 1960.

Ray, Isaac. *A Treatise on the Medical Jurisprudence of Insanity*. New York: Dacapo Press, 1983.

Reisner, Ralph, and Christopher Slobogin. *Law and the Mental Health System, American Case Book Series*. 2nd ed.

Roberts, Patrick. *The Psychology of Tragic Drama*. London: Routledge and Kagan, 1975.

Robinson, Daniel N. Wild Beasts, and Idle Humours. *The Insanity Defense from Antiquity to the Present*. Cambridge, MA: Harvard University Press, 1996.

Romano, John. *Adaptation*. Ithaca, NY: Cornell University Press, 1949.

Rommen, Heinrich A. *The Natural Law*. Translated by Thomas Hanley, 1998 Indianapolis, IN: Liberty Fund.

Sales, Bruce Dennis. *The Trial Process*. New York: Plenum Press, 1981.

Searles, Harold F. *Collected Papers on Schizophrenia and Related Subjects*. Madison, CT: International University Press, 1965. Chapter 8: The Effort to Drive The Other Person Crazy

Segal, Charles. *Tragedy and Civilization: An Interpretation of Sophocles*. Norman: University of Oklahoma Press, 1999.

Simon, Bennett. *Tragic Drama and the Family*. New Haven, CT: Yale University Press, 1988.

Thompson, George. *Aeschylus and Athens The Classic Study in the Social Origins of Drama,* Grosset and Dunlap, University Library, 1968 New York.

Walker, Nigel. *Crime and Insanity in England*. Edinburgh: Edinburgh University Press, 1968.

Wolff, Hans Julius. *Roman Law, An Historical Introduction*. Norman: University of Oklahoma Press, 1951

MacDowell, Douglas, *The Law In Classical Athens*, Cornell University Press

1986, Ithaca NY

Edited by Parkes, Stevenson-Hinde, Marris, *Attachment Across The Life Cycle*, Routledge, London 1995

Bradley, C.S. Watson, *Natural Law, Natural Rights, And American Constitutionalism, Oliver Wendell Holmes, Jr. And The Natural Law*, St. Vincent College

Craig Nelson, *Thomas Paine*, Penguin Books 2007

James Madison, With an introduction by Adrienne Koch, *Notes of Debates In The Federal Convention of 1787*, Norton 1987

Fagles, Robert, translator: *Aeschylus The Oresteia*, Penguin Classics, 1979, pgs. 13-97: A Reading of the "Oresteia"-The Serpent And The Eagle

Cahill, Thomas, *Sailing the Wine Dark Sea, Why the Greeks Matter*, Anchor Books, July 2004

Borden, Walter, *Classically Insane*, Journal of the American Academy of Psychiatry and Law, 39: 2011

Allen, Reginald E., editor: third edition, *Greek Philosophy, Thales to Aristotle*, The Free Press, 1991, New York

Black, Stephen A, *Eugene O'Neill, Beyond Mourning and Tragedy*, Yale University Press, 1999